CW00370105

HEREFORDSHIRE WALKS

Les Lumsdon

SIGMA LEISURE

Wilmslow, England

Copyright ©, L. Lumsdon, 1991

All Rights Reserved. No part of this publication may be reproduced, stored in a retrieval system, or transmitted in any form or by any means - electronic, mechanical, photocopying, recording, or otherwise - without prior written permission from the publisher.

First published in 1991 by Sigma Leisure – an imprint of Sigma Press, 1 South Oak Lane, Wilmslow, Cheshire SK9 6AR, England.

Whilst every effort has been made to ensure that the information given in this book is correct, neither the publisher nor the author accept any responsibility for any inaccuracy.

British Library Cataloguing in Publication Data
A CIP record for this book is available from the British Library.

ISBN: 1-85058-222-X

Typesetting and design by
Sigma Hi-Tech Services Ltd, Wilmslow

Printed and bound by
Manchester Free Press, Paragon Mill, Jersey St., Manchester M4 6FP.

Dedication:
To my parents for encouraging a love of the countryside from an early age.

Acknowledgments:
Thanks go to Hereford and Worcester County Council's Libraries, Rights of Way and Public Transport section, and particularly the Divisional Engineer based in Hereford. Thank you also to the many parish councils and local walking groups, the Association for the Promotion of Herefordshire and Hereford City Council.

FOREWORD
from the
Hereford branch of CAMRA:
the Campaign for Real Ale

Hereford is without doubt the archetype of rural England. When foreign visitors describe the rural idyll that is rural England, they are describing the gentle hills, wild woodland, winding lanes and quiet villages of Herefordshire. This county has a rich history and is fortunately one of the unspoilt corners of Britain, and is full of hidden surprises. Many of the walks will offer the intrepid walker the opportunity to unlock some of the splendid secrets of Herefordshire.

Such beautiful landscape is in danger due to competing demands on that scarce commodity in the British Isles, land. Like the pressures for change on the landscape, another major component of our British Heritage – the pub – is under threat. In Herefordshire, in particular, isolated Inns are often lost forever as holiday homes. Other pubs, forced to make ends meet, take the short-sighted option of throwing five centuries of tradition into a skip to be replaced by bland quasi-restaurants.

Thankfully, all is not gloom and there are plenty of splendid Inns and Pubs in Herefordshire with as much rich tradition as the rural landscape itself. CAMRA is fighting to protect many of these pubs. We recognise these Inns and Pubs are part of the very fabric of our society, and seek to champion them.

The author has laid out an appetising menu of walks which end at many of these very Inns and Pubs. I hope you take this opportunity to enjoy a pint of fine real ale in the pub – after all, it is more than likely the hops have come from Herefordshire. Enjoy!

HEREFORD CAMRA

CHAIRMAN - Mark Haslam

CAMRA HEREFORD can be contacted at:

82, Cotterill Street
Hereford

Tel: (0432) 268486

CONTENTS

Location Plan 7

Herefordshire 9

THE WALKS

1. Bishops Frome	3 mls	26
2. Bodenham	4 mls	31
3. Bringsty Common	4 mls	35
4. Clehonger	7 mls	40
5. Colwall	6 mls	44
6. Craswall	5 mls	49
7. Dilwyn	5 – 6 mls	53
8. Dorstone	10 mls	58
9. Garway Common	4 mls	63
10. Harewood End	5 mls	67
11. Hoarwithy	6 mls	71

12. Kerne Bridge	6 mls	76
13. Kington	12 mls	81
14. Kinnersley	2 mls	86
15. Llangrove	5 mls	89
16. Longtown	3 – 4 mls	93
17. Lugwardine	3 mls	97
18. Mathon	4 mls	100
19. Mordiford	7 mls	104
20. Mortimer's Cross	3 mls	108
21. Much Birch	5 mls	113
22. Orleton	8 mls	118
23. Pencombe	2 mls	123
24. Peterstow	3 mls	127
25. Richard's Castle	3 mls	131
26. Staunton on Wye	6 – 7 mls	135
27. Walterstone	3 mls	139
28. Wigmore	11 mls	142
29. Woolhope	7 mls	149
30. Yarpole	5 mls	155

LOCATION PLAN

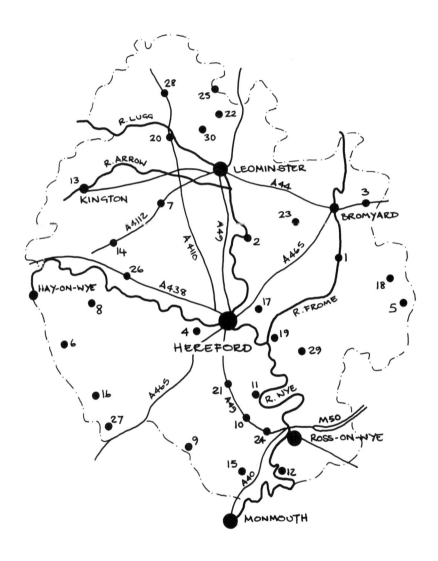

The Old House, Hereford. Photo courtesy of Hereford City Council.

HEREFORDSHIRE

Between the high border ridges of Wales and those majestic Malverns lies the beautiful and ancient county of Herefordshire*. For this oval shaped county, drained principally by the Lugg, Wye and Monnow, offers a variety of landscapes to suit the walker. From the wild windswept commons of Merbach or Garway hill, to the gentle valley bottoms of the Frome and Lugg, it is as unspoilt as the guide books suggest. Only one countryside spot comes to mind where visitors do seem to be thick on the ground – Symond's Yat, on the Wye between Ross and Monmouth. Even here, walk a mile from the Yat and the place is yours. Go elsewhere and the county is empty. Walk on any day except Sunday and you will hardly meet a soul. Apart from the town centres and country parks it is quiet for, regardless of recent trends, many rural Herefordians still live mainly by the land.

The walks recommended in the book vary from short walks (two to four miles) ideal for an afternoon or evening saunter, to longer rambles for those who enjoy being out for the best part of the day. They are spread geographically throughout the county but the reader will notice that in some instances they are clustered together. This allows people who are staying awhile to make good use of the book in one part of the county only. Thus, if camping near The Black Mountains at The Bridge Inn, Michaelchurch Escley, for example, there are three or four walks that can be accomplished without travelling long distances.

Herefordshire Countryside

What makes Herefordshire so interesting for the walker?

---

*Herefordshire is a county that refused to die. In 1974, it became Hereford and Worcester in an administrative and political sense but for all practical purposes, Herefordshire still exists.

In short, the views, for Herefordshire is surrounded by upland masses. In the west there are The Black Mountains, Radnor and Clun Forests. In the east lie the pre-Cambrian rocks of the Malvern hills, and a range of foothills running north to Abberley. In the north, Mortimer's Forest and the Clee Hills come to mind; in the south, the Forest of Dean.

The lowlands of Herefordshire do not appear to be so appealing perhaps. Be re-assured as this gently undulating countryside is broken by lower but nevertheless still impressive ranges such as Dinmore, Wormsley, Merbach and Woolhope, the latter being dome shaped and of considerable interest to geologists. The walks from Mordiford and Woolhope provide a superb introduction to the Woolhope Dome. The county must also have one of the highest number of streams and rivers for such an area. The water and woodland add so much character to the walks particularly in the Llangrove or Clehonger walks.

For the most part the soils of Herefordshire are red. The bed-rock is Old Red sandstone and there have been several periods of glaciation where loams and rich layers have been deposited by melting waters. This has ensured that Herefordshire is a very fertile growing area, in evidence on most of the walks but more so on the Staunton on Wye, Mathon or Bishops Frome walks. In the north west of the county the rock structure, is very different: a series of limestones and shales dating from the Silurian period and the resultant scenery features scarp (edge) and dip (gentler) slopes as on the Wigmore to Lingen walk where buzzards and even the rarer Merlin can be seen. Woolhope also features predominantly limestone rock outcrops often containing fossils embedded for thousands of years in these sedimentary strata.

Early Visitors

Humanity as much as nature shapes a landscape and Herefordshire developed from earliest times as an area of conflict and control. Of the earliest settlers, those hunters and gatherers who took refuge on the high ridges, there is little remaining evidence. Arthur's stone is the most significant find and the walk from Dorstone to Merbach passes by the stone remains of this Neolithic burial chamber. More survives of the Celtic tribes such as the earthworks of British Camp and Croft Ambrey, the former featured in the Colwall ramble and the latter a short distance from the walk between Yarpole and Bircher. There are many other hill fort settlements dating from different times to be seen in the county.

Roman occupation at Kenchester and Leintwardine, linked by the Roman road between Deva (Chester) and Caerleon remind us of the relentless drive to push the Celts west. After the Romans, the story is one of gradual domination during the centuries by the Anglo Saxons and the establishment of kingdoms such as Mercia led to a clearer settlement of territories. Offa's Dyke, a magnificent survival, was one such boundary which straddled the Powys-Mercia border and is featured in the Kington to Lyonshall walk.

Turbulent Past

It is the period before and after the Norman invasion, however, which is so well represented in Herefordshire. Edward the Confessor began to encourage the building of local castles using stone (rather than wood) before the Norman invasion and Richard's Castle, built for Richard Fitz Scrob (hardly a Herefordshire name!), is a good example. Such castles were built for penetrating nearby Wales, if necessary, and the pattern was intensified after the conquest by William the Conqueror. The lands were split between powerful lords, particularly the Fitz Osbornes and Mortimers. The latter family became increasingly influential, ruling much of the Marches (derivation from Mercia) as the area became known, from Wigmore castle. The county is littered with motte and bailey castles dating from this time. Some remain impressive such as Goodrich, others such as Dorstone and Almeley survive only as mounds. War broke out intermittently between these Marcher lords and those who championed Wales as a separate nation, especially the much revered Owain Glyndŵr who was responsible for the slaughter of many Herefordshire armies.

In these few pages it is not possible to chronicle the detailed political and military ramifications of later struggles throughout the centuries as they affected Herefordshire. Mention is made in a more piecemeal way in the description of some the walks. Suffice to say that a pattern of development emerged which has not altered much, even in the industrialised world. For the most part the county began to settle into an agricultural existence and this developed gradually without large industrial incursions on the landscape.

Broad Street, Hereford

Gradual Change

Mills were established on fast flowing streams not only for grinding corn and fodder but for paper and wool. These remained small scale and did not lead to the growth of factory towns as in the North West or Yorkshire. No mining of significance has occurred and even the railways remained on a rural scale. No major direct rail route was forged across the mountains to Wales from the Midlands. Instead, little branch lines were established to such unlikely places as Presteigne and Bromyard. Nor did the canal system stimulate large scale growth as elsewhere. Thus, the county has remained principally agricultural. Even today, two of the county's major employers, Bulmers Cider Company (the largest cider plant in the world) and Sun Valley Poultry are based on processing agricultural produce and others are involved in fruit production in other parts of the county.

Hereford is also famous for Hereford cattle and the Hereford bull is exported throughout the world, the further the better many ramblers would say. The Ryeland sheep is also well known but is not reared extensively. The importance of Hereford and the outlying towns as market places cannot be overestimated and they still retain strong market towns identities. Hereford, while being a cathedral city and major tourist destination, is still first and foremost a place to exchange and buy goods. A visit to the Cattle or Butter market will illustrate this more than words on a page. The county towns of Bromyard, Kington, Ledbury and Leominster still have a special atmosphere. They are quieter, change has been slower, traffic less dominant and tend to feel more welcoming places. Ross-on-Wye is not like the others. It is a more established resort and although the stalls around the ancient market hall and small shops are attractive, the narrow pavements tend to be busier and there is not such a relaxed atmosphere as elsewhere. Don't let this put you off visiting for Ross sits on a site of natural beauty above the banks of the Wye.

Thus, the major changes in the county which have affected the landscape and the culture have come more recently, such as changed farming practices. While less dramatic than in other parts of the country, there has been a grubbing of hedges, and an increase in chicken rearing in large scale buildings which are supplied by equally large lorries trundling down back roads. There has been increased application of pesticides and fertilisers on the land and mechanised harvesting of crops. These farming methods are bringing about a rapid change to the landscape in some parts of the county, and this concerns those seeking to conserve wildlife habitats.

The other major change has been the expansion of road networks and the rise in traffic on major routes, although many back lanes are quieter now then ever before. If ever the A49 becomes the same as the A40 (i.e. an extension of the M50 motorway) the traffic flowing through the county will alter considerably. The move towards greater road building will change the county, as witnessed in other parts of the country and perhaps not wholly a change for the best.

The Villages

It is, however, the villages and hamlets that make walking in Herefordshire such a pleasure. Many have retained a historic charm without becoming genteel. The timber and half timber framed houses in many of the settlements (sometimes called 'Black and White') and a distinctive grouping of buildings around parish churches and village greens make them attractive to the eye. Equally important is the farmyard and home orchard, the post office, pub and local school. Unfortunately, in some parts of the county these are gone. No longer are there pubs at Broad Oak, St. Margaret's or Dulas (what a pub it was!), post offices at Bacton or Bredwardine nor many surviving blacksmiths.

Rural depopulation is not a piece of jargon drawn from a planner's notebook. It is happening every year and, even though sensitive housing schemes have been allowed in many of the villages, young people are not staying and the existing population is ageing. There is no easy answer. Tourism brings a little work and keeps some closer to home but for the most part the trend has not yet been stabilised. Fortunately, many of the communities are host to local groups such as the Women's Institute, Farmer's Clubs and Wildlife supporters and they all bring life to a place.

Weekend Breaks

For those who fancy a weekend away from it all, Country Village Weekend Breaks, pioneered by David Gorvett of Eardisley in the mid to late 1980s is an ideal introduction to Herefordshire – staying with local people in villages such as Brilley, Eardisley, Lyonshall or Pembridge. Pick up a leaflet from a local tourist information office for details. David has since pioneered The Black and White Trail, introducing visitors to the distinctive half-timbered and timbered villages of western Hereford-shire between Leominster and Kington. He has also established a walking trail between the same villages, details of which are also available at local tourist information centres.

Timber framed dovecote, Luntley

Beer, Cider and Perry

Good walking is also about enjoying the local culture and the county of Herefordshire has for centuries been associated with hops and cider. Cider is the beverage well known to Herefordshire and cider apple orchards can still be found throughout the county. Older orchards of standard size trees are, however, becoming rarer. A perry or cider tree may be at its best after seventy years or so growth and some orchards are estimated to be 200-300 years old. Nowadays, most cider producers prefer the faster growing smaller bush varieties with a higher yield per acre and allowing easier picking. Fortunately, a handful of farmers and producers have in recent years planted some of the older varieties and this is gratifying as the old orchard may no longer be a feature of the landscape in the next century.

Many farmers retain an orchard for their own production and towards the back end of the year the crop is harvested and a cider made for family and friends. It is not uncommon to be walking in October or November and come across picking in the orchards either in the traditional way or by something which looks akin to a mini road sweeper.

Real cider is still in production, i.e. cider that is made from crushed cider apples which is then pressed and fermented using few or no additives before being bottled or casked. In contrast, most ciders bought in the supermarkets or your local pub have been filtered, pasteurised or pressurised with carbon dioxide. The larger companies such as Bulmers (market leader) and Westons (fourth largest producer), however, make real cider too. This can be found in some pubs dispensed either by handpump or by pouring from a polypin at the back of the bar! Try it, for the drink is refreshing, with a very fruity taste rather than being sweet and fizzy. Be sure to enquire from the bar staff first as many of the fizzy ciders are branded with the words 'original' or 'traditional'.

Real Perry, a drink produced in much the same way as cider but with perry pears, is a rarity in pubs. There are carbonated bottled varieties but the best perry is produced by companies such as Dunkertons, at Luntley near Pembridge. The Dunkertons have engendered a great interest in traditional ciders and perry. Make a journey to their shop on the premises or to off licences throughout the county to sample their quality products. Be prepared to be disappointed though for perry production has been brought back from the verge of extinction in these parts. There are very few traditional perry orchards left and even though the Dunkertons have begun to plant more trees supply is limited. Westons of Much Marcle also produce a pleasant draught perry, available in gallon jars from their cidery. While in the same village call at Lyne Down farm for a jar of their perry.

Dunkerton's Cider

Farmhouse cider is also produced and sold locally and what better way of sampling than to try a drop after a walk. Do be careful as too much can render the rambler temporarily legless for farmhouse cider gets to the parts that most lagers will never reach! Two such producers are featured in the Richard's Castle (Forge) and Peterstow (Broom) walks. There other producers throughout the county such as Dinmore Farm, Franklins at Little Hereford, Pullens at Ridgeway Cross, Knights at Storridge, Lyne Down at Much Marcle and Great Oak near Almeley. You'll find them selling cider to customers at their premises along with fruit, eggs, honey and home made ice cream in some instances. Some of the producers have joined an organisation, Herefordshire Hamper, which aims to produce and promote good quality produce in the county, everything from cultivated snails to dairy produce or smoked fish and fowl.

Unlike cider the brewing of beer has not been important in Herefordshire. The growing of hops, on the other hand, has and hop yards can
still be seen in the eastern side of the county between Bromyard and
Ledbury. The train journey between Hereford and Ledbury offers the
best view of the hop yards and surrounding farms. Many still have old
oast houses with pointed ventilation cowls where hops have been
traditionally dried before being bagged in distinctive hop sacks. The
fuggle hop is still used by some brewers in making traditional beers and
thus has secured a future for a smaller number of hop growing farmers.

During the past two decades the county has been dominated by one
brewing giant, Whitbread. This company has been criticised for buying
up smaller brewing concerns, closing their breweries and selling off less
profitable public houses especially in rural areas. One of the main critics
has been The Campaign For Real Ale (CAMRA) which has been fighting
for choice of real beers in pubs which are still as characterful as their

The Barrels, formerly The Lamb Hotel

local communities. The local CAMRA group can be contacted at CAMRA Hereford, 82 Cotterill Street, Hereford; Tel: 0432-268486.

In recent years, the situation has improved dramatically in Herefordshire for many public houses released by Whitbread have become free of brewery tie and sell a range of real beers from several breweries. Thus, it is possible to buy a pint of Brains, Hook Norton, Smiles and Wood in Herefordshire nowadays where little was previously available.

The second encouraging development has been the success of The Wye Valley brewery in St. Owen Street, Hereford which sells good tasting beers at the brewery tap, The Barrels (formerly The Lamb), and in the free trade. The area around St. Owen Street is fast becoming a mecca for traditional brews. Next door to The Barrels is a lovely old pub, The Sun, where real cider is dispensed from wooden casks on the bar and pale ale drawn from the deepest cellar in Hereford. You are guaranteed a frosty pint in mid winter and cool glass when it is scorching outside! A few steps along, opposite the fire station is The Jolly Roger (formerly a Whitbread pub, The Bricklayers), something of a theme pub, but selling beers brewed on the premises and also real cider.

Country Pubs

Walking and pubs go very much together and fortunately there are dozens of good country pubs to choose from in Herefordshire. You may be seeking pubs not changed much this century such as The Hop Pole at Risbury, The Carpenters at Walterstone or Cupid's Hill Inn just across the border on the road to Grosmont. Alternatively, you may seek more food-based pubs such as The Angel at Kingsland or the New Inn at St. Owens Cross. Most have retained a charm and provide a warm welcome. A superb companion is 'Real Ale and Cider in Herefordshire' by Ian Wraight and Mark Dyer, available at the following address by post, price £1.75 plus postage (say 50p):

Mark Dyer
43 Nicholls Lane
Winterbourne
Bristol
BS17 1NG

Most of the pubs included in this guide serve real ale and many offer a traditional cider. Remember that most pubs survive by selling food as well as drinks so publicans generally do not allow you to consume your own food on the premises. Children, (well behaved ones), are almost always welcome at lunchtimes and early evenings and there are often seats outside. Publicans tend to dislike boots, especially if muddy and cannot accept dogs for hygiene reasons. Given these provisos, walkers tend to be most welcome.

Opening hours are always a problem but generally speaking, most of the pubs mentioned are open at weekday lunchtimes, and many remain open all day on Saturday. Several pubs are closed on a Monday or Tuesday lunchtimes, particularly in the winter. Wherever known, the author has included this sort of information to avoid disappointment.

Pubs do add to a country walk, so enjoy yourselves en route or at the end of a ramble.

The Old Hop Pole inn, Risbury

The Wye and Hereford Cathedral

The Walks

A few years ago the mention of walking in Herefordshire would have brought a smile to the face for many of the footpaths would have been obstructed or in severe neglect and used only by those with local knowledge. The mood is changing. The County of Hereford and Worcester, in liaison with parish councils and voluntary groups, are re-opening and improving paths. There's much to be done but walking in Herefordshire is now a serious proposition. No longer are you confined to certain spots in the Wye valley, to The Malverns or localities in the Woolhopes. Paths are being opened in parish after parish, stiles repaired, wooden signs and waymarks provided so that the walker is more confident about the route to take. These facilities are for resident and visitor alike and if there is mutual respect between rambler and landowner the position can only improve.

Travel and Refreshment

Wherever possible it is best to travel to the villages by bus, bicycle or train in some instances. In this way you avoid parking problems, put money into local facilities and can sit back and enjoy the scenery more. The bicycle has to be the most environmentally sound option and cycling around Herefordshire can be a real joy if you keep off the main roads.

Local bus information leaflets are available at libraries or by contacting the Public Transport Section at:

Hereford and Worcester County Council
County Hall
Worcester WR5 2NP
or by 'phone
(0905) 766799 (Monday to Friday 0830-1730)
(0432) 356204 (Monday to Saturday 0900-1700)

In the same way, suggestions are made about where local refreshment and provisions can be bought in the villages. In this way you give back something to the host community. A village shop, for example, might be saved from closure if visitors use it.

Practical Guidelines

The rambles were researched during the summer and autumn of 1990 and any minor problems referred to Hereford and Worcester County Council. The paths should be clear but if you find any major problems let the Rights of Way Officer, County Hall, Worcester WR5 2NP know about them so that others will not be hindered. Many of the local paths are surveyed by The Ramblers Association which has done sterling work in campaigning for a better footpath network. Get in touch with your local group by way of The Ramblers Association, 1-5 Wandsworth Road, London SW8 2XX. Tel: 071 582 6878

Most of the walks are suitable for families and in some instances cut off points are suggested should those little legs become tired after a mile or two.

The directions should be sufficient to allow the suggested route to be walked successfully but many people like to use an Ordnance Survey Pathfinder map as well, given the amount of detail shown on these sheets. Virtually all the walks involve climbing stiles of some description. The term 'stile' is used generously as they come in all shapes and sizes, from a few pieces of wood nailed together to a gap stile between gate posts. Directions are given assuming your back is to the stile every time you cross a field boundary. Some paths have been waymarked with little yellow arrows and the walker will find this most helpful.

Changing World

The environment is changing constantly. After all, this book is about walking through a working landscape. One year a field can be under an arable crop, the next sown with winter grass. It is potentially more confusing when woods are chopped down or hedges grubbed. Thus, the description might ask you to walk alongside a hedge that no longer exists. For such matters an apology is issued in advance and future editions will introduce the necessary revisions.

A few matters do worry people when they are out especially when walking areas of mixed farming. People sometimes hesitate when they find a crop of cabbages or rape seed oil planted in a field and with no path re-instated. This should not be the case, of course, as it is a crop obstruction and the path should be re instated for the walker. It is your right to proceed on the right of way without impediment and if plenty do this the path will soon be trodden down. This is easier said than done if children are with you and you might simply wish to walk the field edges to regain your position at the other side.

Bulls

Bulls are more problematic. Many a farm hand has been known to be trampled by the very bull they have looked after for years. So avoid walking near any bull regardless of what the regulations say about which ones are docile. There's always one bull to disprove the general thesis. As with an obstruction simply find the nearest alternative route around the field in question and regain your path.

Don't forget that this is a working countryside so expect to find lanes very muddy after rain and inquisitive cows seeking fodder in winter. Sometimes bits of barbed wire are put up to stop animals and not people from damaging hedges. Worse for the rambler is the low level electric wire used to cordon animals in fields, many of which happen to be level with or an inch below the crutch. Look for a gap or where the wire is lowest as the shock is a little stronger than a tingling sensation (He said in a high pitched voice). Considerate farmers usually put a piece of insulated tubing for walkers to get over at a certain point.

Two criticisms tend to be aimed at ramblers. One is litter, so please ensure that it all goes home with you, even orange peel and the like. By the way, you'll come across tipping of rubbish in holes and sunken lanes on some of the routes, old cookers and cars, hardly the sort of thing lugged about by the rambler. On a more serious note, concern is expressed about dogs worrying cattle and sheep so if you do have a hound please keep it under control and where there are animals, on a leash. Fouling of pavements and paths in and around villages is another problem area which heats up the debate.

Lastly, make sure that you wear suitable clothes in case the weather changes. Boots are better than wellies or trainers although the latter are comfortable in dry summer months. A small knapsack with a drink, snack, first aid kit and a waterproof is not much to carry and ensures that you have some back up if things go wrong.

Most importantly, enjoy your walking in Herefordshire.

Key to maps

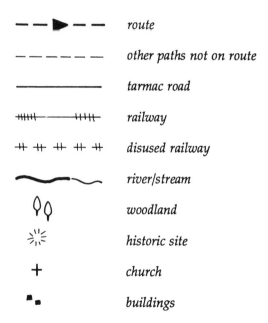

route

other paths not on route

tarmac road

railway

disused railway

river/stream

woodland

historic site

church

buildings

1. BISHOPS FROME

A walk along paths to Halmonds Frome and The Majors Arms, a very hidden part of the county. Good views and some steady climbs.

Distance: 3 miles

Map: Pathfinder sheet 1018 Great Malvern

How To Get There:

By Bus: There is a Monday to Saturday service between Hereford, Bishops Frome and Bromyard

By Car: Travel on the A4103 road between Worcester and Hereford turning onto the B4214 to Bromyard at Five Bridges for Bishops Frome. There is very limited car parking in Bishops Frome.

Refreshment: Those who enjoy real ales will become quite excited in the village of Bishops Frome. Both the Green Dragon and Chase Hotel offer a range of draught beers from all over the country and offer good food into the bargain. The Majors Arms at Halmonds Frome also offers Marstons real ales and guest beers. The core of this sixteenth century pub was originally built as a cider mill and is open at lunchtimes throughout the week. Ideal for the walker as it re-opens at 5pm on Mondays to Fridays and welcomes families. What better place to be on a summer's day? Make sure the driver stays on fruit juices or better still plan a trip by bus then everyone can imbibe in safety. Afternoon teas are available at The Hop Pocket Craft Shop in Bishops Frome.

Nearest Tourist Information: Council Offices, Rowberry St, Bromyard HR7 4DX. Tel: (0885) 482431.

Bishops Frome is a large village for these parts and this, no doubt, relates to its sheltered position above the confluence of the Filly brook and River Frome. It is also because of the area's hop growing tradition. The large number of hop yards in the area meant that every year an army of pickers would come to stay and they would require food and drink and more drink at the end of each day. There are fewer hop yards now and a reduced number of orchards in the area but agriculture is still a major business activity.

The name, Bishops Frome, presumably derives from the river itself like sister villages such as Canon Frome and Castle Frome, the latter having the earthworks of an old castle a fine Norman church. These lands in

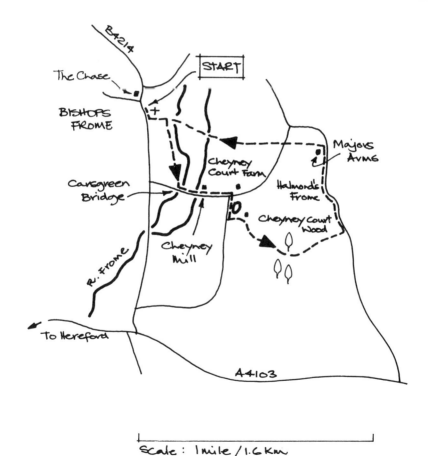

Scale : 1 mile / 1.6 Km

early medieval times belonged mainly to the church and hence the name Bishop, referring to the Bishop of Hereford at the time.

The ridge running south from Bromyard to Stanley Hill overlooking the Frome valley makes for splendid walking and what better introduction than a circular walk to Halmonds Frome, a lovely venture on a summer's eve when the sun is setting over the valley.

Bishops Frome church

Start from The Chase Hotel. Follow the main road around to the right by the church and go left through the churchyard as signed to a kissing gate leading to a bridge over a tributary of the River Frome. Do not go over but turn right instead to follow a path along the field's edge to a tarmac lane. The church is on slightly raised ground which is a possible indication that it could have been a prominent Anglo Saxon site. Not much remains of the original Norman structure but inside there is an interesting font and effigies of one-time local notables.

Cheney Court

Turn left and follow the lane over Cansgreen bridge and by the old Cheney mill on The Frome. At the junction before Cheyney Court farm turn right and then within a short distance turn left through a gate into a field with a pool to the left and farm buildings ahead. One of these is thought to have been a chapel. The stone mullioned windows can be seen clearly and the size of the structure lends itself to the argument. The chimney is of a later date than the rest of the building. The pool might well have been part of a moat around the court.

The track leads to the back of a barn where you turn right to go through a gate and then climb up the field with the hedge to the right. Keep ahead, making your way towards the top field corner and Cheney Court wood pausing now and again to look back over Bishops Frome. Before the corner cut left across the field to enter the wood and walk along a sunken track heading slightly left uphill and to a field's edge. As the old track is virtually blocked by fallen wood here, walk along the edge of the field to a gate ahead. Go through it and keep ahead to exit onto a tarmac lane by a cottage.

The Majors Arms

Turn left and follow the road to the Majors Arms with a humorous ditty on its wall:

'This is the place
That hinders none
Eat and drink
And travel on'

Just below the pub is a path to the left leading down the field through rough pasture. Cross the stile at the bottom, cross the road, go over the stile next to the cottage and follow the narrow green lane down to another stile. Cross this and walk through a small paddock to a gateway, then head slightly right across the field to cross a stile in the corner. Head slightly right to cross a footbridge over the infant Frome and keep ahead to the church by way of another footbridge. Having explored two of the Fromes do not forget to take a look at the others on your next visit.

2. BODENHAM

An easy ramble along clearly marked paths in a quiet part of the Lugg valley returning to Bodenham church which is overlooked by the wooded slopes of Dinmore.

Distance: 4 miles

Map: Pathfinder sheet 994 Leominster

How To Get There:

By Bus: There is a Monday to Saturday service to Bodenham from Hereford. Ask for Bodenham Memorial.

By Car: Travel on the A49 road north and as you approach Dinmore hill turn right for Bodenham. Turn right at the Memorial stone and there is car parking near to the church.

Refreshment: The England's Gate public house

Nearest Tourist Information: St Owens Street, Hereford, HR1 2PJ. Tel: (0432) 268430

Bodenham village has grown in the lowlands around the River Lugg as it winds is way around the spur of Dinmore hill. For those who enjoy a more energetic walk there is a path up from Bodenham to Queenswood visitor centre at the top of Dinmore by way of Henhouse (no clues for guessing the derivation of this) and Church coppice standing high on the ridge. The ramble suggested here, however, is more of a summer saunter, a stroll across the fields to relieve the cares of the world and sip some of Herefordshire's softening atmosphere before returning home for tea or supper.

Broadfield Court

Whilst discussing soothing qualities, on the Risbury road up from Saffron's Cross and the Isle of Rhea is Broadfield Court: a historic estate which cultivates its own vines and produces a good bottle of Bodenham Reichensteiner for the table. Tours of the vineyard can be arranged for groups and there are periodic open days for the public. Check with Tourist Information, however, before travelling.

Effigy

Most of the settlement in recent years has occurred between Bodenham Moor and England's Gate rather than around Bodenham church. This causes some confusion to those travelling to the village for the first time, for the village is now quite spread out. The walk features the old village, between Bodenham Bridge and the church, lies the village cross and alongside a more recent war memorial. The church itself is, however, a focal point and can be seen for the most part of the walk, its solid tower adorned with a small spire. Take a look inside as there is a particularly moving effigy of a woman and child thought to date from the fourteenth century.

Start the walk from The Memorial. Turn right, heading in the direction the newer part of Bodenham village and the River Lugg. Cross the Bodenham Bridge and turn next right along a quiet lane. Mid way look for a stile on the right and cross it. Head slightly right walking in the direction of Bodenham church. Cross a stile beneath an oak tree and proceed slightly right again through a gap in the hedge (look for the waymark post) and then cross another stile in the next boundary to approach the river bank.

Follow the Lugg around to the footbridge but do not cross. Instead, head slightly left across this large meadow to a footbridge over a stream and Ashgrove wood and ridge to the left. Follow the hedge on the left to the next boundary. Turn right after the gap and go ahead to another gap and old gate.

Proceed ahead along the field's edge with a hedge to your left around to a house known as Vern cottage. A stile leads out onto a lane. Turn right and walk along the access road towards The Vern. However, turn next right along a track which gives out into the large field with which you are now quite familiar. If you are wondering what the water is on the other side of the Lugg they are gravel pits which have been a source of employment locally and, to many, an irritation for many years.

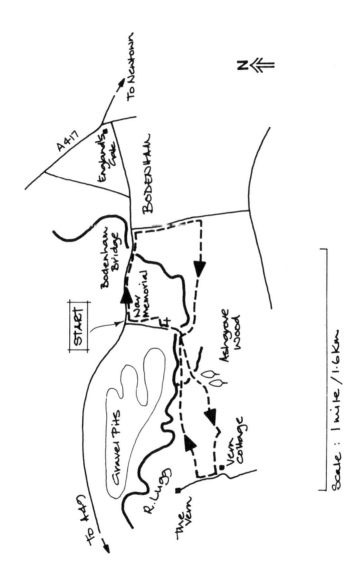

Scale : 1 mile / 1·6 Km

River's Edge

However, the return crossing of the field is shorter as you keep ahead to a double stile and then a footbridge. Walk ahead once again along a strip of rough grass to the river's edge. Turn right and follow the river back to the footbridge at Bodenham. Is this not a poetic setting?

Cross the bridge and enter the churchyard leaving by way of the lych gate. Turn right and then left to return to the Memorial. Not far away is England's Gate. For those wishing to combine the ramble with a visit Queenswood or Dinmore manor gardens, they are only two miles or so away.

Queenswood offers an information centre, shop and cafe in recently restored and distinctive timbered framed buildings as well as dozens of short walks through the woods and country park. In the direction of Hereford is Dinmore Manor where the gardens, chapel, music room and cloisters are open to the public. The latter was established by Richard Hollins Murray earlier in this century, the inventor of the ingenious cats' eyes, found in the middle of major highways.

3. BRINGSTY COMMON

A different walk featuring common, paths and tracks by farms and cottages in this well known beauty spot.

Distance: 4 miles

Map: Pathfinder sheet 995 Bromyard

How To Get There:

By Bus: There is a regular Monday to Saturday bus. Ask for the turning to the Live and Let Live public house near Bringsty Common post office.

By Car: Bringsty is on the A465 from Hereford to Bromyard and then the A44 between Bromyard and Worcester. There is car parking in and around the picnic area by the pub direction sign to the Live and Let Live public house by the side of the road.

Refreshment: The Live and Let Live public house, a fascinating old pub which was once a cider mill still serves a good pint of traditional cider but made by Bulmers rather than on the premises. It is well off the beaten track and difficult to get to by car. There is also a cafe at Bringsty garage less than half a mile along the A44.

Tourist Information: Council Offices, Rowberry St, Bromyard, HR7 4DX. Tel: (0885) 482341

Bringsty Common is not far from Bromyard Common and both are popular on warm summer Sundays. For the rest of the time Bringsty common is yours to roam in virtual solitude. This bracken covered open land is undulating and dotted with old cottages and pockets of orchard. The swathes of bracken are broken by clear green paths and tracks and rights of ways to from the common are mainly clear. Those who argue that there is no need for commons in the latter part of the twentieth century ought to visit more places like this, for not only are they places of recreation but also refuges for wildlife. Thanks go to campaigners such as the Open Spaces Society for their continuing hard work in

The 'Live and Let Live'

saving commons for our enjoyment. A well written book 'Access to The Herefordshire Countryside Today' by Jenny Minton is a great introduction to Herefordshire commons so add it to your Christmas list this year.

Depending on your tastes, the highlight of the walk will either be the views across to Whitbourne hall or when you finally get to sit down at the more humble Live and Let Live. The journey to Bringsty can be combined with a visit to Lower Brockhampton, a fourteenth century timbered house with surrounding chapel and buildings, owned by the National Trust and open to the public on certain days. It lies between Bromyard and Bringsty.

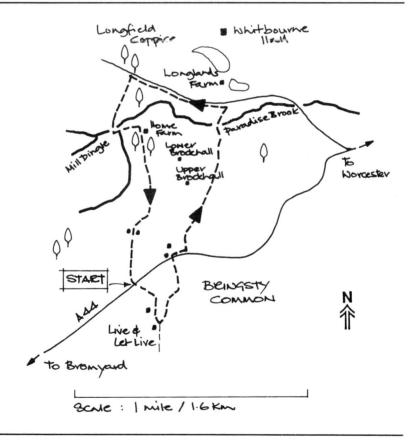

Bromyard

Walkers might also choose to call into the nearby town of Bromyard with half timbered shops and inns not much altered over the decades. Bromyard has a sound reputation for its May day events and folk festival held later in the year. It attracts local farmers from the surrounding district on market day, Thursday.

Start the walk from the turn on the right to the Live and Let Live public house. Walk down the track with farm and orchard to the right and the Live and Let Live along the next track on the right. However, if saving your call until later turn left up a steep green path between bracken. This path leads back down to the road which you cross by the cottage and turn right to walk to the corner almost opposite a disused chapel overgrown by nature on the right. Go left across the common and head straight down the track to the corner where you cross a stile into a field.

Cut across the field left, to go over another stile and head down the valley as it curves left, with views across to Whitbourne Hall ahead. Go through the gate and keep ahead a short while until you come to a footbridge on the left. Go over it and to the gate on the right. Once through, follow the track up the bank to the tarmac lane.

Whitbourne Hall

Turn left here, but your eyes will be on Longlands farm in the foreground and Whitbourne Hall beyond with its classical Ionic front standing out boldly amongst the trees. This was the work of Elmslie in the 1860s, an architect who had something of a passion for classical Greek as did the owner, Edward Evans who made a fortune out of vinegar and wine but not in the same bottles. He travelled throughout the world on the profits but his true love was Greece.

Follow the road to a bluff above Paradise brook offering good views over to Home farm, which you will be passing shortly. The road straightens and Longfield coppice is to the right as your turning is left, signed to Old Mill cottage.

The lane leads to it, presumably an old mill by the brook in years gone by. Follow the track as it curves around left, through the orchard to

Home farm with a hedge on your right. Go through the gate by the farmhouse with dogs barking and geese hissing, no doubt as you walk through the farmyard to go through a gate on the right leading into another orchard. Please be considerate when passing through.

Walk up the bank and cross a stile on the left just beyond a gap. In the next field continue up the hill with a hedge on the right. Go through a gap and keep to the hedge on the right which leads to a stile beneath a very old oak. Walk up the narrow green track flanked by holly and between cottages onto the common. Take the middle green track and head for the picnic area by the main road.

4. CLEHONGER

The ramble between the large village of Clehonger, the hamlet of Ruckhall and Eaton Bishop includes such a variety of scenery from common to riverside, through sheltered valleys and open fields that the walker will hardly notice the miles go by.

Distance: 7 miles

Map: Pathfinder Sheet 1040 Hereford(South) and area

How To Get There:

By Bus: There is a daily bus between Hereford and Clehonger but the Sunday service is less frequent

By Car: Travel on the A465 road between Hereford and Abergavenny and at Belmont turn right onto the B4349 to Clehonger. There is some parking available in and around the main road in the village

Refreshment: The friendly and well-run Steven Stars at Clehonger sells Whitbread draught beers. The Ancient Camp Inn (referred to by locals as The Camp without the 'ancient') at Ruckhall is a free house with plenty of seats outside to admire the spectacular view. The emphasis in recent years has been on food. There is a shop and garage at Clehonger.

Nearest Tourist Information: St. Owen Street, Hereford HR1 2PJ. Tel: (0432) 268430

Clehonger is a divided village, one part surrounding the church seen on the journey out of Hereford and the other the larger community a mile away which has grown up to the south of the main road. The Seven Stars lies between both parts and even the old stores and post office is a little removed from the nucleus of population. Thus, in many respects the village has outgrown its traditional boundaries.

You may have also noticed Belmont Abbey and school. The former was designed by a famous architect, A. W. N. Pugin in the last century, who is perhaps better known for his work in designing part of the House of Commons. While in the area, Pugin must have wandered along to Clehonger church for it is reckoned that one of the stained glass windows is his work too. The church, of course, is much earlier with several surviving Norman pieces of architecture and there are several well-preserved monuments and brasses inside.

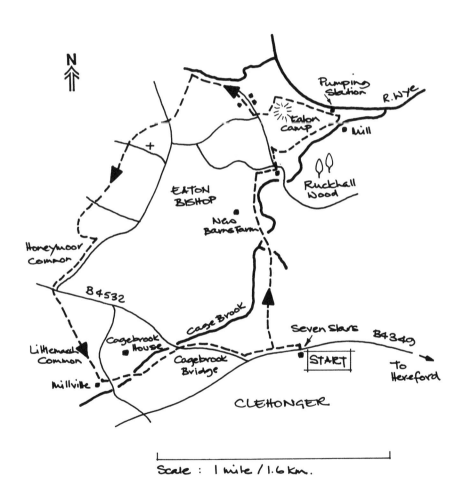

Scale : I mile / 1.6 km.

Cage Brook

Start the walk from The Seven Stars at Clehonger. Turn left and walk along the main road into the village. After the garage and before the stores go right over a stile and head downhill slightly right, with good views of The Bines and Cage Brook, to cross a stile. Keep company with the hedge on your left in the next field and cross the stile on the left. Do not be put off by the rhythmic thumping of the water pump below. Walk down to the right of the pump house, cross the sleeper bridge and then turn left through wetter ground to meet a bridge over the brook.

Turn right and go over the wooden rails in the fencing, now walking ahead along a shoulder of the bank, the austere looking New Barns farm up top to your left, to cross a small stream by way of a sleeper bridge and then a stile. Keep ahead across the field to a gateway and into the tarmac lane. Turn right and then next left before Ruckhall mill where flour was once ground. This is quite a climb so stop for a breather and turn next right along a track which gives great views of Ruckhall. As this track veers left to a house go down a narrower path, sometimes a little overgrown, which winds down beneath the old orchard trees. Look out for a right hand fork descending to a stile which you cross and then turn left to cross another stile and onto an aggregate track.

Notice the old water mill and works to the right and the earthwork remains of Iron Age ramparts. The track leads left by the pumping station and then up steps and through the wood. Unlike years ago, there are now signs to direct the rambler past the Ancient Camp Inn.

If you are not stopping for food and drink continue along the bracken clad path for a short distance before it turns left up to a lane. Cross here and walk up the green lane to a junction where you go right. At the road go right and then left. This road leads to Brooking cottage where the path is to the right over a wall. This path winds around to a low fence which you cross. In the field, turn right and follow the field's edge a short distance until you see a footbridge on the right. Turn left here to cross the field along a worn path. Cross the stile and continue over a short section of field to a road. Turn right and immediately left over a stile. Walk up the field to cross another stile by a barn and then walk up the right hand side of the paddock to cross two stiles and onto a track.

Eaton Bishop

To the left is Eaton Bishop church of Norman origin and with some very fine stained glass windows thought to date from the fourteenth century. Cross the track and the stile. Go slightly right in this field with views over to Madley church and the Black Mountains beyond, and the telecommunications dishes at the old Madley aerodrome. Cross another stile and keep company with a hedge on the right. Go over another stile and walk alongside a hedge crossing two stiles guarding a sleeper bridge. Keep ahead to the next gateway and then cross a track and another stile. Go slightly right to cross another stile and now walk with the hedge to your left and onto Honeymoor Common.

Turn left and follow the track to the road then turn right, although some ramblers might wish to cross the common, which can get wet, more directly to the road junction with the main B4352 road. Cross the road and go over the stile into a large field. Head slightly left towards a wood at Littlemarsh Common, tucked away in this quieter part of the parish. A stile leads into the common and as the path is not clear here keep ahead through wet ground into an open space and a tarmac lane. Cagebrook House stands to the left, a proud looking Georgian building

Turn right and follow the lane down to a right corner but you go left over the stile and then right to follow the field's edge alongside the old mill and leat. This path is waymarked with yellow markers and leads into a 'Site of Special Scientific Interest' – so please keep to the footpath and do not touch plants or foliage as the path leads over the footbridge into a beautiful wood rich in flowers and wildlife. The path is less clear as it moves away from the stream, sometimes broken by fallen trees, but for the most part follows the bottom of a slope before exiting at a stile on the main B4352 road.

Turn right and walk up the hill into Clehonger village.

5. COLWALL

A climb up to The Malvern hills and to The British camp returning by way of Evendine along paths and tracks to Colwall. The views are exhilarating, the breeze refreshing and your pulse rate will be racing.

Distance: 6 miles including the last climb up to Herefordshire Beacon

Map: Pathfinder Sheet 1018 Great Malvern

How To Get There:

By Train: There is a daily service between Hereford, Ledbury, Colwall The Malverns, Worcester and onto Birmingham. The Sunday service starts in the afternoon.

By Car: Travel on the A438 to Ledbury then the A449 towards Great Malvern but then take the B4218 to Colwall Stone. There is parking near to Colwall station.

Refreshment: There are several public houses and shops in Colwall. There is a cafe on route and The British Camp hotel so there's not much chance of missing refreshment if needed. The CAMRA recommended pub in Colwall is The Chase at Upper Colwall. The pub does not allow children.

Nearest Tourist Information: The Winter Gardens, Grange Rd, Malvern WR14 3HB. Tel: (0684) 892289.

Colwall is perhaps best known as a place where mineral water is bottled by the 'schh...you know who' company and also as being the one time home of romantic novelist and poet Elizabeth Barrett Browning. It was in Colwall that she was crippled by a spine disease possibly as a result of a riding accident at the age of fifteen. In her confined existence here and later in London she wrote much of her best material. One London admirer was the poet Robert Browning who eventually became her husband and took her to Italy for the remainder of her life.

Colwall has also been home to Jenny Lind, the nineteenth century singer sometimes called the Swedish Nightingale, reflecting her place of birth and popular singing talents.

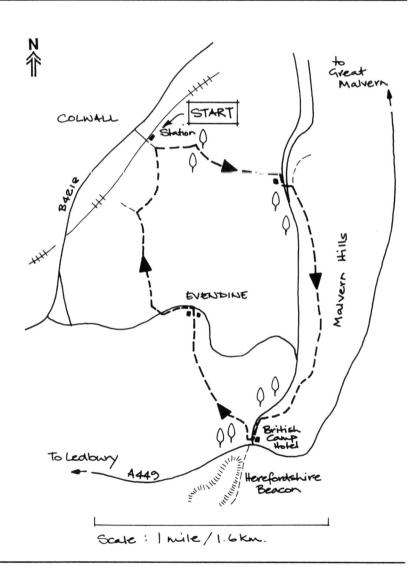

Scale : 1 mile / 1.6 km.

The village has in the past been a hive of small business activity including a strong local reputation for vinegar production. It is more of a dormitory area now. The older part of the parish is situated around the church a mile or so away.

Local WI

Start from Colwall station. This little unstaffed station (for most of the time) has been tidied up in recent years by the local WI group. It's a real asset to Colwall, not only for the commuter but also for those who wish to go shopping further afield. The line has survived and is now championed by The Cotswold line promotion group which exists to encourage the fullest use of the Oxford to Hereford route. Details of the group can be found in their lively newsletter which is available at locations in and around the line.

Walk over the footbridge, along a path to a gate leading into a field and go left along the field's edge and up to cross a stile in the top left corner. Begin to climb the wooded slope zig-zagging across other tracks but heading in a slightly right direction up the bank. There is no real landmark but keep across the field to a stile to the right of three trees. Walk up the green lane but be vigilant, for part way up you cross a stile on the left and then turn right. Keep company with the hedge to your right, cross another stile and walk up to a tarmac lane. You can go directly right here if calling at 'The Kettle Sings' tea room for a break.

If not, head up the lane to cross the main road and slightly right through the car park and climb up the hillside once again to join another path. Simply continue up the hill until you join a main path and turn right. The views are magnificent across Herefordshire to Oyster hill in the foreground and to the Woolhopes beyond.

The Malvern Conservators

Keep ahead as the path descends, avoiding lesser paths off to the right or left. Join another main path and bear right again descending and then as it begins to curve right join another path descending at a gentler pace down to a car park. Cross this and you will notice as at the previous car park that the bye laws and car parking ticket machines refer to The Malvern Conservators, a committee established to preserve the Malverns for visitors and residents alike. Sounds simple enough but the issue stirred the emotions during the last century.

The major landowner in these parts was Lady Foley, a woman said to have been very much like Queen Victoria in manner and circumstances. Her estates were vast and she was certainly not keen to allow encroachment of Malvern common land for building or other purposes by anyone else but herself. She also felt that preservation of the hills should be on her own terms. One opponent was Stephen Ballard, who lived to an equally ripe old age. He engineered the Colwall railway tunnel under the Malvern hills and was a vitriolic critic of Lady Foley and those who stood with her in the debate. She, by the way, refused to travel by train through his tunnel because she thought it was too dirty.

Green Tourism

Reasoned argument prevailed, however, and by 1884 Parliament passed The Malvern Hills Act establishing a Board of Conservators to preserve common land for the thousands of visitors who came by train as well as the residents. This early example of Green Tourism, recognising the need to manage demand at this growing national resort of the time, has continued ever since. Many of us still come by train but the conservators seem more concerned about controlling cars a hundred years on.

British Camp

Walk over the hillock ahead and back down to the main road to turn left to the British Camp hotel. For those wishing to continue, cross the road and follow the well-worn path up to the British Camp, also called the Herefordshire Beacon. This is a magnificent earthworks said to date from 100 BC and reckoned to be one of the many attributed to the warrior leader Caracticus. If he did live in all these camps his life must have been hell. The circumference of this camp alone is estimated at one and three quarter miles enclosing a considerable acreage. The earthworks are in good order and it is easy to imagine how impressive a defence it would have been with wooden pallisades. Is this the place where Caracticus stood for the last time against the imperialist Romans?

On a more peaceful note it is thought that the wandering fourteenth century poet William Langland was inspired by a dream while on these very hills which led to the writing of the delightful 'Vision of Piers Plowman'. Slumber or not, retrace your steps to the hotel, cross the road and pass by the toilet block to start the return section to Colwall which is far easier going than the first part of this ramble. The path drops down over a rough grass bank to a large field and then crosses it to a stile. Keep ahead to cross a bridge and a stile and proceed along the field hedge to your right until it cuts away to the right. Continue ahead to a gate leading into a track between houses and to a road.

Evendine

Turn left and pass the interesting Upper House and Malt House in the hamlet of Evendine, as pretty a place as it sounds. Follow the road around left and then look for a little green path leading up to a stile on the right. Cross it and another virtually in succession, then go across the paddock to a stile. Cross this and exit onto another track by way of the stile next to the gate. Turn right and follow the track to a stile leading into a field. Keep ahead for a matter of thirty paces or so then cross a stile on the left where a well worn path leads across this field slightly left to a stile which you cross. Walk ahead with the hedge on your right but at the next boundary go right through the gateway and keep company with the hedge on your left through a gateway and to cross a stile in the corner. Cross this and then go right over a stile and to the gate leading back to the railway station.

6. CRASWALL

Hill walking mainly along a bridleway but also over moorland returning by way of a lane. Plenty of climbs and not a place to be in winter when the weather is rough.

Distance: 5 miles

Map: Pathfinder 1039 Golden Valley

How To Get there:

By Bus: There is a very limited service from Hereford to Craswall Post Office, approximately two miles from The Bulls Head public house.

By Car: Travel on the Hereford to Abergavenny A465 road and turn right up to Longtown and then left in the village before the Crown inn. After a mile, at the next main junction take the right fork and follow the road to Hay-on-Wye for approximately three miles. The Bulls Head public house appears on the right. There is a limited amount of roadside parking before the pub and a little further on, near to Craswall chapel.

Alternatively, Travel by way of Hay-on-Wye, taking a left turning off the Talgarth road, B4350, onto to the road for Capel-y-ffin and Llanthony. A good mile out of Hay take the left fork for Craswall and Longtown.

Refreshment: The Bulls Head, a modest pub of yesteryear frequented mainly by farming people. It sells a lovely pint of Westons cider and snacks are available. Stone flag floors, old settles and other rustic features make the place seem timeless. There is also camping available in a nearby field.

Tourist Information: Hay-on-Wye: the Car Park, Oxford Road, Hay, HR3 5AE. Tel: (0497) 820144

Start the walk from the Bulls Head in Craswall, an isolated public house on the road to Hay. From the entrance turn left and within a very short distance turn right up a bridleway leading uphill to a junction. Turn

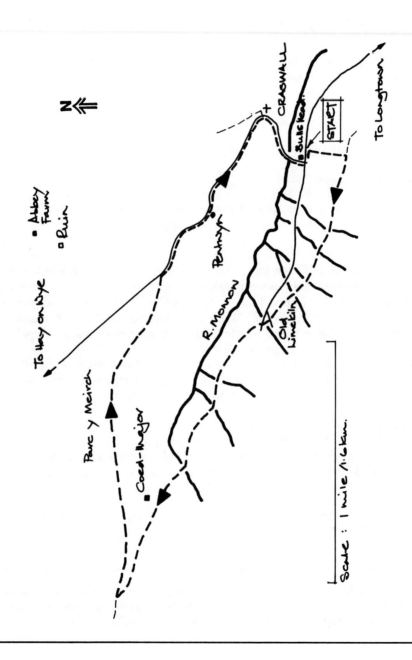

right here joining another bridleway coming from the Olchon valley. The path is well used and by horses too so expect it to be muddy after rain. In places it is distinctly a track, in other parts less clear. However, it more or less follows a straight line along the edge of the upper reaches of the Monnow valley to a watershed.

Bubbling Brooks

At first the track is green and tree lined. Pass through several gates and across infant bubbling brooks. It narrows to a path alongside a tall hedge and ahead to another gate. Proceed ahead and soon walk through a short field to another gate. Go through it and cross another stream and gate. Shortly, you come to a junction of tracks surrounded by a patch of fern. The way is ahead to a stream, then right and along a path to the left of a tarmac lane. Cross the track and keep ahead again.

The bridleway begins to climb more steeply now as the valley narrows with several small waterfalls as the streams cut down to harder bands of rock. Pass through a wider section with sheep pens and then descend to cross a ford before zig-zagging right and then left with a hedge to your right. The view back over this hilly part of the county is excellent.

The softer terrain gives way to moorland now with wetter ground and plant life more akin to such an altitude, sheep looking scraggy. Proceed ahead as you climb out of the dip, keeping the fence on your right as a guide. Pass by Coed-major farm and a recently planted area of woodland.

Turning Point

You come to a junction, the turning point of the walk in more ways than one. Go right here, with a drystone wall to your left. Go through the gateway, now heading back along the ridge with the farm now to your right. Keep to the hedge on the left and once past the farm go through another gateway. Do not stay on the main track. Go slightly right by two gateposts and then keep ahead, through the gate in the fence. Go across windswept moorland to another gateway and then shortly cross a track. Keep ahead to walk alongside a hedge on the right towards the corner of the field. As there's no stile here, cut across to the barred gate which leads onto the road.

Craswall Abbey

To the left across the fields is Abbey farm and the ruins of Craswall abbey, a monastic institution established by the rare Grandmontine order. Founded in the early thirteenth century and abandoned two hundred years later, it is amazing how much of the ruins still stand five centuries later. There is a path up to the ruins from Craswall church, mentioned below.

Turn right and follow the lane as it winds down into the valley, passing Craswall church, an isolated place of worship for the scattered congregation. Just before the church is a bridleway path leading off from the corner of the road up the Monnow valley to Craswall abbey.

The sting in the tail for the rambler is the last sharp climb up to the pub but do not fear, refreshment is near.

7. DILWYN

Gently undulating countryside with recently improved footpaths, a mile or so of lane walking linking two delightful villages on The Black and White Trail.

Distance: 5 to 6 miles

Map: Pathfinder Sheet 994 Leominster

How To Get There:

By Bus: There is a very limited bus service from Hereford and Leominster to Dilwyn. However, it is far easier to travel to Weobley and the walk can be started from the latter place quite easily.

By Car: Travel on the A4110 Hereford to Knighton road. After Bush Bank look for a left turn at a crossroads signed to Dilwyn. There is a small amount of on street parking available in the village.

Refreshment: The Crown Inn, a comfortable old village pub, serves Whitbread beers. There are also tea rooms and inns at Weobley.

Nearest Tourist Information: 6 School Lane, Leominster. Tel: (0568) 6460

Dilwyn's green is a real feature in this village with the pub and Dilwyn stores on one side and restored half timbered houses on the other; at one time farm buildings, a reflection of changing times and ways of life. Just up the road stands the church in a commanding position overlooking the village and Dilwyn Common. Dating from Norman times but with much restoration since, the church is well loved by the community.

There are several interesting features including the key to the south porch which is 17 inches long, a record for the county if not elsewhere. The church bells, forged by the once famous Rudhall company at Gloucester contain several inscriptions including the matter of fact:

'I to the church the living call
And to the grave do summon all'.

The Marches Tour arriving at Weobley

Earthworks

Start the walk from the entrance to The Crown. Turn left and left again
away from the village green and shortly turn right by the fine looking
Georgian Townsend House. The road descends gently and as you
approach the houses on the right, turn left over two stiles and along the
edge of the field to a footbridge. Cut across the field to a stile which you
cross and then keep ahead with the hedge to your left to cross another
footbridge. There are earthworks to your right, presumably an old
fortified building at one time.

Head slightly right across the field to meet a stile mid way along the
hedge opposite. Cross this and then keep ahead across another large

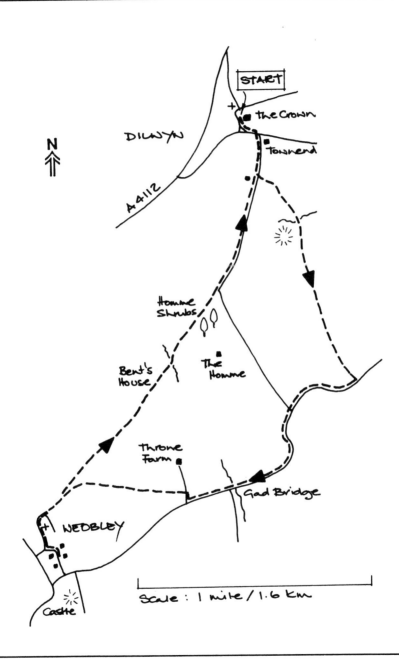

Scale : 1 mile / 1.6 km

field to a gate leading into a lane. If in crop there is a track a little to the right and then a re instated path mid field as shown on the pathfinder.

Throne

At the road turn right and follow this for half a milc to a junction by a house. Proceed straight ahead and then follow the road down to Gad Bridge. Keep ahead again and climb up gently to the turning for Throne farm on the right. The reference to the word 'Throne' refers to a time when the farm incorporated an inn where King Charles I, in the days of The English Civil war, stayed before fleeing his pursuers.

Turn into the drive but immediately cross the stile on the left and follow the narrow path to cross another stile beneath the electric telegraph pole. The distant outline of Weobley church spire, the tallest in the county, can be seen more clearly now as you approach the village.

Cross the field ahead, go through a gap in the hedge and walk along the edge of the field ahead to cross a stile into an orchard. Cross another stile and proceed through the barred gates and left along the track towards Weobley. Turn second left by the church and left again into the village centre.

Weobley

Weobley has always been a place of interest. The conservation of many half timbered and timbered houses throughout the village has been admired throughout the ages. Weobley is probably quieter now. It once despatched two members to Parliament as it was a Borough of considerable import in political terms or, at least, the local nobility were well connected. This was stopped by the Reform Act of 1832, the first of a series of acts during the nineteenth and early twentieth centuries to make the electoral system more democratic.

Weobley attracts far more visitors than Dilwyn, so it is that little more commercial. One of the nicest ways to arrive is in a Marches Tours vintage Bedford coach from Ludlow and Leominster, the sort of vehicle that Wye Valley Motors thrived on after the Second World war. The coach can often be seen parked up for an hour or so during the summer months while people browse around Weobley's characterful streets.

Spend time to look at the earthworks of Weobley castle just behind the centre and there are several local walks to Garnstone Hall, once the home of Colonel Birch, a famous Parliamentarian in the English Civil war. The hall is in ruins and Colonel Birch lies in the graveyard of Weobley church which also contains monuments to other notables in the community.

Retrace steps back to the lane beyond Weobley church but now go through a gateway onto a bridleway with the hedge on your right. Go through a two gateways between fields and soon you will see The Homme to your right and Dilwyn church ahead in the distance. Go through a third gate to pass the scant remains of Bent's House and a barn. Bent would be disappointed if he could see what's left of his place. The track dips slightly left to a bridge and then climbs gently between oaks to a stile by a gate adjacent to a wood named Homme shrubs.

Walk ahead with the wood to your right and then cut slightly left to a gateway and onto a road. Follow this for half a mile into Dilwyn, turning left to the village green. Slumber under the village green trees or take refreshment at The Crown after the walk for Dilwyn has a relaxing air about it.

8. DORSTONE

A strenuous walk from the pleasant Golden Valley village of Dorstone to high Merbach hill by way of Arthur's Stone, an ancient burial chamber. This ramble includes several steep climbs and should not be attempted in poor weather conditions. There is three mile of walking along quiet hill top lanes but not all in one section.

Distance: 10 miles

Map: Pathfinder Sheet 1016 Hay-on-Wye

How To Get There:

By Bus: There is a Monday to Saturday service between Hereford, Hay and Brecon calling at Dorstone.

By Car: Take the A465 to Belmont, turn right onto the B4349 to Gooses Foot to join the B4348 to Dorstone.

Refreshment: The Pandy Inn, Dorstone. This exceptionally friendly pub in the centre of the village serves Bass, Boddingtons, Brains beer and good food. It is thought to be the oldest pub in Herefordshire, built by Richard de Brito in 1185 to house workers while building Dorstone church (see below). It is said that Oliver Cromwell supped here between battles in and around the county. The pub, hosted by Chris and Margaret Burtonwood is more relaxing these days. The pub is sometimes closed Mondays and Tuesday lunchtimes in winter.

There is also a village store and the lovely Pump House Tea rooms nearby so refreshment and provisions are catered for.

Nearest Tourist Information: Hay-on-Wye across the border in Wales. The Car Park, Oxford Road, Hay-on-Wye, Powys HR3 5AE. Tel: (0497) 820144.

Dorstone is a large village in the western end of the Dore valley so its name is easy to work out. The area is known as the Golden valley which

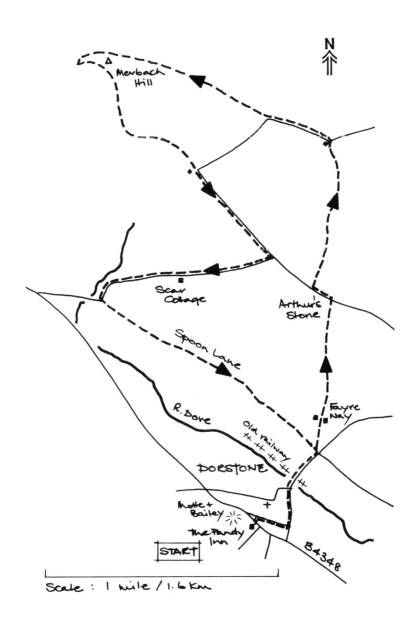

N

Merbach Hill

Scar Cottage

Spoon Lane

Arthur's Stone

R. Dove

Old Railway

Fayre Nay

DORSTONE

Motte + Bailey

The Pandy Inn

START

B 4348

Scale : 1 mile / 1.6 Km

presumably could be a rough translation of the French word d'Or meaning gold. This was possibly a mix up over the Welsh word Dwfr referring to water. Regardless of derivation the name is very apt for whatever the weather the gentle valley always seems to be bathed in warm sunlight. While here travel down the valley, which is ideal cycling country, to Snodhill castle, Peterchurch village, Urishay farm museum and tea rooms and, further south, Abbeydore and Bacton. They are delightful places. The loveliest has to be Vowchurch and Turnastone, hamlets nestled on opposite side of the Dore. The names, so they say, come from two sisters one of whom exclaimed in anger one day:

'I vow I will build my church before you can turn a stone of yours'.

Golden Valley Railway

It has always been one of the remoter parts of the county and is to this very day. The nearest that Dorstone has come to being opened to the wider world was when the Golden valley railway was built in the late 1870s. The local notable, Lady Cornewell cut the first sod at Peterchurch in 1876 and this very rural railway from Pontrilas to Hay-on-Wye tottered into existence. As one can imagine, the expected revenues were grossly overestimated and between 1881 and 1889 the trains terminated at Dorstone while the track was put down to Hay. Thus, by the end of the century the Golden Valley railway was in trouble and the acquisitive Great Western railway bought it lock, stock and barrel for £9,000 compared with the estimated investment of the past twenty years of £334,786. This not only hurt community pride but dozens of local business people in a financial way. Sad to say the last passenger train left Dorstone on 17 August 1950 with school children bound for Porthcawl and the line was then gradually dismantled during the early 1950s.

Dorstone Village

Dorstone village centre is very pretty, with the sundial and old cross on the village green and lanes radiating to all parts of the community between old houses. Behind the Pandy inn are the earthworks of a motte and bailey castle which was governed by the Solers family in succession to the Mortimers. There is no stonework remaining, so the castle will no doubt be well represented in walls and buildings for miles around.

There is an intriguing history of the village published by the Dorstone Village History Committee in 1990 to celebrate a centenary of the restoration of the church. This successfully attempts to paint a picture of Dorstone during the past hundred years. Try to get hold of a copy for it will make the visit more enjoyable.

Start at The Pandy Inn, Dorstone. Walk to the right of the green triangle and sundial in the village square and turn right along a narrow road by houses. At the next junction go left down to the main road. Keep ahead, across the old Golden valley railway. Dorstone station would have been to the right and a level crossing existed at this point. Walk up to the corner, crossing beforehand as it is hazardous.

Just beyond a track to the left, shown as a 'No Through Road', is a gate ahead, leading into a field with a stream to the right. Walk up this field to pass between a new farm house and Fayre Way. A Hereford guide book dating from 1931 describes this as a 'greenway' and in many respects the clear route can be discerned although fewer walk it than in previous decades. Keep to the hedge on the right as the old track rises to the next gate. Go through it and left uphill and through two more pastures and gateways keeping the hedge to your left.

Arthur's Stone

Once through the latter gateway follow the indent of the old track mid field to Arthur's Stone, a neolithic burial place dating from approximately 3000 BC which would have been much bigger than the stone slab remains seen now. It is the only significant find of this period in the county. Evidently, up until the last century it was the scene of annual festivities and Pagan worship around the stone. One couldn't imagine a colder place in winter.

Turn left here and follow the tarmac lane ahead for a short distance. Around the first gentle bend, go right through a barred gate. Follow the track ahead to proceed through another gate. Walk ahead again, to the left of the trees to pass through another barred gate and then walk down the field's edge, to cross a stile into the next field. The path descends slightly left alongside the wood to meet a track passing by a house to a lane. Go left here, up the hill and as the road curves sharp left continue along a track and onto Merbach Common. The path leads ahead through bracken and climbs gently at first. It then narrows and steepens to a triangulation point amid old quarry scars. The views across Wales and to the Midlands are excellent. On a warm day it is an exhilarating place to sit and view the world below, to watch the clouds sweep over the meandering Wye and to feel the breeze ruffle your hair. What a sense of freedom!

Rested, turn left at the trig point in an easterly direction to a small gate leading into a field. Keep ahead following the line of hawthorn bushes and then a hedge as it curves gently towards a house on your right. Exit onto the lane and walk back to the T junction where you turn right. The lane drops steeply in places by Scar cottage winding down to the valley below. As it levels look for a track leading off left, known as Spoon Lane. This is well worn at first. It gets rougher half way along but then becomes a clear route again as a farm access track leading to Dorstone.

Walk back down the main road possibly returning by way of the churchyard for this restored church houses the tomb of a murderer, Thomas de Brito: one of the three knights who wilfully executed Sir Thomas-a-Becket in Canterbury cathedral in 1170. He repented his sins in the Holy land before returning to these parts to atone even further by building the church. What store of history lies in this little known parish.

9. GARWAY COMMON

A very remote part of Herefordshire with views across the Monnow valley to Wales. The paths are not clear on the ground but this circular route is passable. There are a few climbs so make sure you have been training.

Distance: 4 miles

Map: Pathfinder sheet 1064 Ross-on-Wye (West)

How To Get There:

By Bus: There are buses from Hereford to Garway Common on Monday to Saturday but mainly on Wednesdays, Fridays and Saturdays. One travels in a circular to Kentchurch making for a scenic ride out.

By Car: Travel on the A49 south from Hereford then turn right onto the A466 Monmouth road to just beyond Saint Weonard's, where you turn right onto the B4521 to Abergavenny and in one mile turn right at Broad Oak to Garway Common. There is limited car parking around the common near to The Moon inn.

Refreshment: The Moon inn which has a small bar area and a lounge restaurant is an amazing survivor in this sparsely populated area. It usually has one or two draught beers brought in from afar so is of interest to those who enjoy a real ale or two.

Nearest Tourist Information: St Owen Street, Hereford, HR1 2PJ. Tel: (0432) 268430.

Garway, Garway Hill and Garway Common are wild places, known to Herefordians but not much visited. Locals at Wormelow say that the frontier post is Orcop Hill probably as many get waylaid at the Fountain Inn. Geographically, the area is a rolling plateaux, a watershed between feeder brooks of the Garron and Monnow mainly. While Garway is very much in England today this was not always the case. In past times the community was predominantly Welsh speaking. So much so that the church had to be careful which clergy to send to this parish and on some occasions English speakers were despatched, much to the surprise of parishioners and priest alike.

The population has declined considerably and given this and the rise of car ownership, local shops and other facilities have gone except the church and inn. You'll not come across many walking these paths but it is an area worthy of exploration.

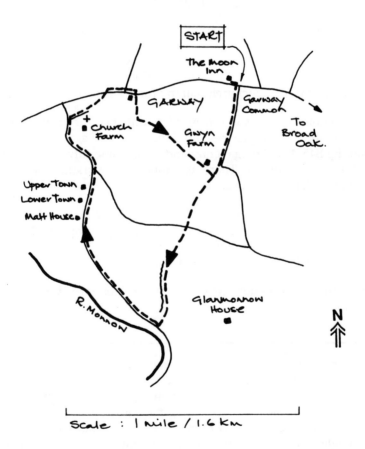

Scale : 1 mile / 1.6 km

Start from the entrance of The Moon. Turn left and then right through Garway Common, past some houses and then, as the road bends sharp left, go through a gate ahead and continue down the field with the hedge to the left. In the bottom left hand corner cross an awkward stile which leads onto the road.

Birds of Prey

Cross the stile on the other side and continue to walk down this field with a stream to your right and Glanmonnow house up on the hill. This is the land of the buzzard which can often be seen and other birds of prey. The path exits by way of a stile onto a tarmac lane. Turn right and begin to climb towards Garway church. The lane is often host to violets, stitchwort, campion, wood anemones, cowslip, yellow nettle and vetch adding colour where you would not expect it. Pass Lower and Upper Town and meet another lane coming in from the right. Follow the lane to the left of Church farm and then turn right along the track to the church itself.

Knights Templar

The church is large for the population of the parish. In mediaeval times, the land in these parts was owned by the Knights Templar and they invested in Garway church. The remains, exposed by excavations in 1927, of a round nave can be seen and are thought to be of the twelfth century. Head for the top left corner of the churchyard and exit into a field but before proceeding take a look at the splendid round dovecote in the farm beneath the church. This was also built by the Knights Templar and holds an amazing 666 nesting places. Head slightly right across the field climbing to Garway Cross to go through a kissing gate onto the road.

Turn right and just beyond the road junction on the left and cottage on the right go right, through a barred gate and follow the field's edge to a barred gate ahead. Go through it and follow the hedge once again until you reach a gate on the right. Turn left at this point and head across the field with The Gwyn farm as a landmark in the distance. Go through the gate between a cropped and tall hedge. Cross a stile and keep company with a hedge to your left at first but then keep ahead as it falls away left, aiming to the right of the farm buildings. Pass to the right of the farm and at the far end turn left to retrace your steps back to The Moon. Sometimes it is pleasant to sit outside and watch a game of cricket on the common or simply ponder over the dilemma of English clergy spreading the good word to a Welsh speaking worshippers. This is borderland country.

10. HAREWOOD END

Easy walking between Harewood and the Wye valley at Hoarwithy using old bridleways, tracks and paths.

Distance: 5 miles

Map: Pathfinder Sheet 1064 Ross-on-Wye (West)

How To Get There:

By Bus: Harewood End is served daily by the Hereford to Ross-on-Wye and Gloucester bus, 38, including journeys on Sunday afternoons.

By Car: Travel on the A49 road to Harewood End.

Refreshment: The Harewood End inn serves real ales and food and The New Harp in Hoarwithy supplies Whitbread draught beers. They both offer food. Alternatively, bring a bottle of Chianti, garlic bread and tuna pasta for at one stage in the walk you could well believe you are in Italy.

Nearest Tourist Information: 20 Broad Street, Ross-on-Wye Herefordshire HR9 7EA. Tel: (0989) 62768

Harewood End is a group of dwellings around the old coaching inn which also doubled up at one time as a magistrate's court. One can imagine how interesting the judicial decisions might have been as the day wore on. The area is characterised by a large amount of parkland as is Pengethley. Harewood hall, however, unlike Pengethley Court has gone, although the old lodge can still be seen on the main road at Windmill hill.

Start the walk from The Harewood End inn. From the entrance turn left and go left along a track which soon becomes a narrow bridleway. This leads to a gate and exits onto an aggregate farm track ahead. Follow this to Woodlands farm where you proceed through the farmyard. Then, go through the gate on the left and follow the track around to the right. Go through another gate with Lower Horse rough to the left.

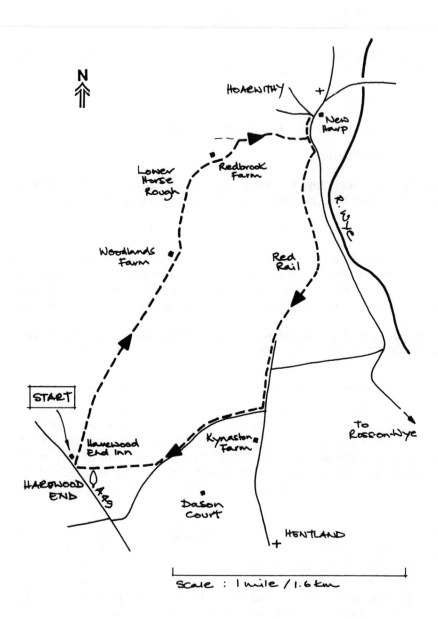

N

HOARWITHY
+
New
Harp

Lower
Horse
Rough

Redbrook
Farm

R. Wye

Woodlands
Farm

Red
Rail

START

Harewood
End Inn

HAREWOOD
END

A49

Kynaston
Farm

to
Ross-on-Wye

Dason
Court

HENTLAND
+

Scale : 1 mile / 1.6 km

Italianate Style

There's a superb view across to the Woolhope Dome from here and also of Hoarwithy village and church. The Italianate style of the church seems to blend so well with the surrounding environment. Many comment that the village looks Italian from a distance on a sunny Summer's day. The church is not much more than a hundred years old and was built on the site of earlier churches. Take a look at it when in the village.

You reach a gateway at the end of the wood which you go through and then descend slightly to the right to pass to the right of Redbrook farm. Join the track coming in from the left and this brings you to a tarmac road. There are good views of How Caple church along this section. Turn left for the village, a snug settlement nestling beneath a bluff above the Wye. It has always been something of a crossroads and crossing point for the river. In the recent past camping has become more popular in the area and keen local walkers inspect the footpaths so most paths are clear and easy to follow. Whatever the purpose of your visit The New Harp is friendly enough, being one large bar now rather than two in the past.

Stilts

On the return leg, turn left out of The New Harp and walk a short distance along the road towards Ross. Just beyond the route where you entered the village look for a path on the right leading uphill between trees. Climb this to cross a track and a stile by a gate to enter a field. Pause awhile to take a look over to the graceful River Wye and to Sellack church. Near to this is the Sellack footbridge which allowed villagers to walk between Kings Caple and How Caple without an exhaustive detour. It was certainly welcomed by one reverend at the time, for this determined man is said to have used stilts to cross the Wye rather than walk miles upstream!

Walk through this long field keeping company with an old hedge to the right. In the corner cross a stile by a gate and follow the hedge to another stile by a gate. Cross this and climb to meet another track. Continue ahead to the tarmac road.

Hentland Church

At the next junction turn right. The road ahead leads to Hentland church, dating originally from the thirteenth century but having been extensively restored in 1853. It remains a pretty wayside chapel for use of the local court.

The lane climbs steadily and after the turning for Dason Court on the right look for a stile on the right as signed. Head slightly left across this field to cross another stile. Keep ahead in the next field in roughly the same direction to a stile leading into Harewood End wood. This cuts across the wood to a house and garden where the path exits onto the main road. However, most people turn left before the garden to go through a gap to the roadside at this point. Is it time to retire to make judgements at The Harewood Inn?

11. HOARWITHY

A walk in one of the prettiest parts of the Wye valley to an equally delightful inn, aptly named the Cottage of Content. Return along the banks of the Wye to Hoarwithy village. One climb at the start of the walk, otherwise gentle terrain.

Distance: 6 miles

Map: Pathfinder sheets 1040 Hereford South and 1064 Ross-on-Wye (West)

How To Get There:

By Bus: There is a limited Monday to Saturday bus service to Hoarwithy from Hereford and Ross-on-Wye.

By Car: Travel on the A49 from Hereford and after The Axe and Cleaver at Much Birch take the next turn left at Cross Collar crossroads to Hoarwithy village. There is limited on street parking near the church and by the bridge on the Fawley road but please park considerately.

Refreshment: The New Harp at Hoarwithy: see Walk 10. The Cottage of Content at Carey serves a lovely pint of Hook Norton beer brewed at a traditional Victorian tower brewery in an equally beautiful setting in the Cotswolds. The pub has retained a public bar area and a lounge, and is well known for its good food. Not open Monday and Tuesday lunchtimes in Winter. CAMRA recommended.

Nearest Tourist Information: 20 Broad St, Ross-on-Wye. Tel: (0989) 62768.

Start the walk from the gates of the church dedicated to St. Catherine, an Italian style red sandstone building dating from the 1880s which seems to fit so beautifully into this Hoarwithy hillside. Climb up the road in the direction of Hereford out of the village and then turn right into a quiet back lane which leads through a farmyard. As the road curves

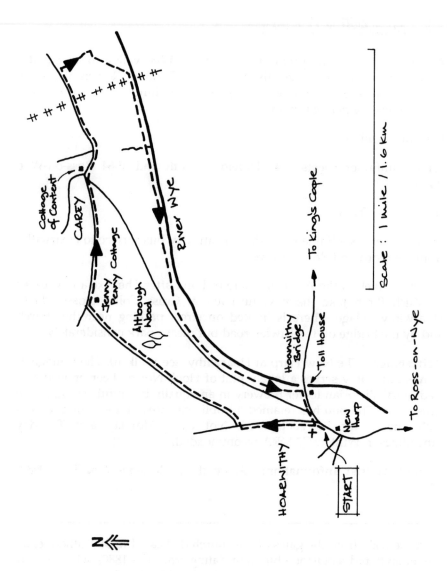

right keep ahead along an old hedge track which rises above Altbough woods to a crossroads.

The Cottage of Content

Turn right here and walk down the hill, past Jenny Penny cottage and Whitehorn wood to Carey. Just as you are beginning to tire, the hamlet surrounding The Cottage of Content inn, comes into sight as you meet another road coming in from the right. Keep left, cross the bridge and rest awhile at what has to be one of Herefordshire's prettiest pubs. It was not always so, having been labourers cottages before becoming The Miners Arms and since 'The Cottage.' Carey must be one of the county's smallest hamlets with no more than a dozen houses in the locality, less than in previous centuries.

Gloucester Railway

If continuing, rather than stopping at the pub, follow the road around to the right and by cottages at Rock farm, passing a junction to the left. Follow the road beyond the old trackbed of Hereford and Gloucester railway with a view of Ballingham old station. This line was closed in the 1960s under the Beeching regime as part of drastic economy measures. Just think of the tourism potential now if it were still open. A group of supporters plan to develop at least part of the line as a leisure railway but they face a colossal task. If it were not to be a steam railway wouldn't it make a superb traffic free cycle route from Hereford to Ross and perhaps through to Huntley or maybe along the old line to Monmouth and Chepstow.

Beyond the old railway the road curves left and then right. Look at this point for a green lane off to the right. This leads into a field where you follow the field's edge around to a stile which you cross. Walk beneath the abutments of the railway bridge. On the other side is the entrance to the old Fawley tunnel which led to Fawley station, now a private residence. The old station inn, The British Lion, has survived however and is still very much a basic friendly country pub selling real beer from the Wye Valley brewery. It is only a few miles from Hoarwithy by way of King's Caple.

Riverside Path

The rest of the walk is simple. Follow the banks of the Wye through a succession of fields until you reach a tarmac lane. Go left along the road at the beginning of Hoarwithy village but within a short distance cut off left again along a path by the river. This leads a short distance to the new Hoarwithy bridge. The first one was of wooden construction dating from the 1850s but this was replaced twenty years on by a structure which survived until the late 1980s when it was closed for a complete rebuild. This caused considerable consternation as a journey to the doctors became a twenty mile run rather than a mile across the river. One or two began to use boats again to make the passage across the river as would have been the case in earlier centuries where the Wye shallows here.

The building by the bridge, if you had not guessed by now, is the old toll house and given its position it would have been hard for anyone to

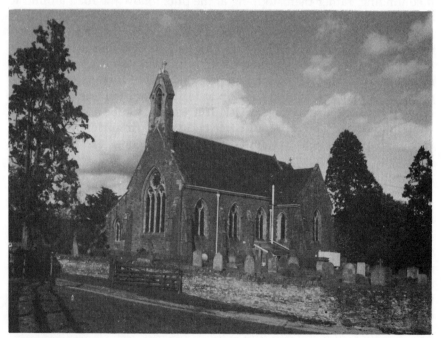

Little Birch church

sneak by. Toll houses were common on bridges across the Wye, the only remaining charge being made at the Whitney-on-Wye toll bridge near Hay-on-Wye. Their design has tended to be functional rather than aesthetically pleasing but these toll houses do have character. Turn right for the village.

Hoarwithy is well used by walkers and the paths are clear. There is a superb walk to Sellack bridge and church by way of Ruxton and King's Caple returning by way of Red Rail. There are also lovely walks by Tresseck and Prothither mill to Little Dewchurch or Little Birch so a return visit is more than likely.

12. KERNE BRIDGE

Not for the faint at heart for this walk includes several climbs and the hardest comes at the very beginning. The views make for considerable recompense and there's a gem of an old world pub half way round. There is also one in Kerne Bridge, so you won't go thirsty on this great outdoor venture.

Distance: 6 miles

Map: Pathfinder sheets 1064 Ross-on-Wye (West), 1087 Monmouth

How To Get There:

By Bus: There is a regular service from Ross-on-Wye, services 35 and 61 on Monday to Saturday

By Car: Travel on the B4228 from the centre of Ross-on-Wye or from Hereford on the A49 and A4137 to Whitchurch, then the B4229 to Kerne Bridge. There is car parking and a picnic site by the bridge alongside the River Wye.

Refreshment: Kerne Bridge inn, Castle View Hotel at Kerne Bridge and the New Buildings public house at Bulls Hill. The Kerne Bridge Inn offers varied guest beers from throughout the UK, and serves bar meals. Your host, John Martin-Slater also arranges weekend breaks, and the pub is CAMRA recommended.

Nearest Tourist Information: 20 Broad Street, Ross-on-Wye HR9 7EA. Tel: (0989) 62768.

Kerne Bridge, dating from 1828, has been described as a fine long bridge across the Wye and has given its name to the surrounding settlement. Previously, travellers had to cross the river by a nearby ferry. Legend has it that one famous passenger in 1388 was Henry IV who was met here by a messenger in a great hurry to announce that a son had been born unto him at Monmouth: the son who would grow up to be Harry of Monmouth or Henry V. The King was so pleased that he gave the ferry and its earnings to the ferryman to be passed on to his children and theirs.

Flanesford Priory

Kerne Bridge is also one of the last places on the Wye where coracles are made and seen. Across the river is the remains of Flanesford priory, tastefully incorporated into holiday apartments at a farm. The priory belonged to an Augustinian order who settled in these parts during the fourteenth century.

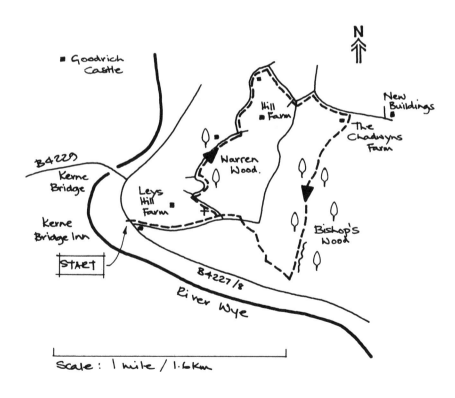

Goodrich Castle

Beyond on the hillside is the majestic Goodrich castle, a fortress built in red sandstone during the latter part of the eleventh century by Godric Mapplestone. It remained as a castle through the centuries up to the English Civil War when it was held first by the Parliamentarians, then by Royalists under the command of a Sir Henry Lingen. He held out under siege for some time before being overpowered by cannon, mining and constant barrage. It is open to the public and the ruins are well preserved.

Start the walk by the Kerne Bridge inn. Walk up the steep back lane leading off from the main road behind the inn. This winds up the hillside in a steep gradient so don't feel embarrassed when gasping for breath by some of the roadside dwellings with views across the Wye valley to Coppet Hill and to the Forest of Dean.

In approximately half a mile, turn left along a concrete access road between houses leading towards Leys Hill farm. Pass an old chapel, Old Chapel House and then soon afterwards turn right before Leys Hill farm along a dirt track leading up to join another track. Go left here for the length of the adjoining paddock and then turn right along a delightful woodland path to pass by a house and onto a track once again which curves right to leave the wood.

Glorious View

Turn left at the junction here and walk down the lane as far as the corner where you take the path off to the right but only for a very short distance for at the next corner cross the stile on the left into a field with a glorious view of the Wye valley with the village of Walford in the flood plain below, the wooded Chase bluff and Ross-on-Wye beyond with the tall spire of St. Mary reaching towards the sky. Don't rush this part of the walk for the view, especially on a summer's eve, is one to be savoured.

The well worn path leads down the field to a gate just to the left of a distinctly red brick house. Turn right here and walk along the tarmac lane for a short distance to pass a small building on the right and to approach a house on the left. Go right through the barred gate at this point and through the gap on the right into the next field, (although a new stile could well be in situ by the time the reader attempts this walk). Then turn left and climb up the bank to cross a stile, through another field and through the gap and onto a gate leading onto a track. Go left here and left again at the next junction.

The New Buildings

After a short stretch, turn right at the next junction to walk along the road passing a telephone kiosk and corrugated iron bus shelter and descend the valley of Bishop's wood with The Chadwyns farm to your right. You turn right down a track just past the farm but, if you are in need of refreshment, continue along the road ahead to a T-junction and The New Buildings public house comes into sight. This charming rural pub lost in these hills and run by a delightful landlady is well worth a visit. It is usually open at lunchtimes at the weekend only. Retrace steps to the turn by Chadwyns. Follow this track down to a point where it

The New Buildings Public House

curves left and follow the path which leads off into the wood and make sure you have a stick to hand to cut back the voracious bramble. As the path drops the brambles disappear and it becomes a very pleasant meander along the stream to woodland cottages.

Continue ahead along the track almost to the main road with the left and right track system before you. Go right here up a narrow walled track by barn and allotment. Turn right at the next junction and left shortly afterwards. This exits onto a drive by a cottage. Keep ahead up to the tarmac road where you turn left for the heavenly descent to the Kerne Bridge Inn.

13. KINGTON

A great walk full of interest, between a market town and historic village on The Black and White Trail. There are a few climbs but for the most part they are not strenuous.

Distance: 12 miles (Can be made into a 7 mile ramble – see *How To Get There* section)

Map: Pathfinder Sheet 993 Kington

How To Get There:

By Bus: Kington is served by a regular Monday to Saturday bus from Hereford. Most of these pass through Lyonshall as do the Kington to Leominster buses so it is possible to catch the bus to Lyonshall and walk back to Kington if a shorter ramble is preferred.

By Car: Kington is on the A44 from Leominster and the A438 then A4111 roads from Hereford by way of Eardisley. There is a car park at the back of the Market Place off High St.

Refreshment: There are cafes, take-aways and several pubs in Kington. The Royal George in Lyonshall serves Whitbread beers. Church House in Lyonshall specialises in Victorian afternoon teas.

Nearest Tourist Information: Information Office, Council Offices, 2 Mill St, Kington. Tel: (0544) 230202

Kington is a border town lying between Hergest Ridge and Bradnor Hill and the confluence of Back Brook and the River Arrow. It is surprising that there is not the ruins of a major castle here as in earlier times the Kington folk took sides with the Welsh as well as fighting for the English Marcher Lords. There are very scant earthworks near to the church which is situated prominently on the road to Hergest Croft Gardens, well loved by visitors and locals for its blaze of colours in springtime.

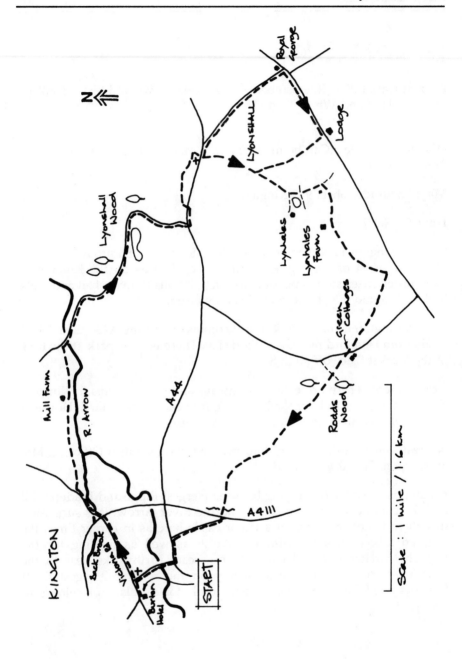

Black Vaughan

In the church lies the tomb of Thomas and Ellen Vaughan of Hergest Croft. It is said that Thomas Vaughan's spirit in time gone by has scared both man and beast and was known as Black Vaughan. Things got so bad that people stopped coming to market here so the town's elders brought in a group of clerics to remove the spirit. That, they managed but only just, and legend has it that it has since lain at the bottom of a pool on Hergest Ridge. Even spookier is the story of the haunting black bloodhound at Hergest Court which is said to have been the inspiration of Sir Arthur Conan Doyle's 'The Hound of The Baskervilles'.

It seems that Kington folk were a little on the pugnacious side for in the early 1820s many were involved in the Rebecca Riots where men dressed as women, darkened their faces and then ransacked local toll houses, causing the local constabulary a puzzling problem.

Wordsworth

The main street, High Street, leads into Bridge Street and Victoria Road with its small shops and market taverns. There's a lovely feeling about the town and some very interesting architecture if one looks closely. For some time, Wordsworth lived near the centre but he did not wax lyrical about the place in comparison to the Lake District or Tintern. That might be a blessing!

Start the walk from the Burton Hotel by the Market Hall. Walk along the main shopping street, High Street and into Victoria Road to the roundabout and by pass. Leave by the road on the opposite side signed to Presteigne. Proceed, facing the traffic, with Back Brook between you and the industrial estate. Note the remains of the old Kington station on the line from Leominster to New Radnor which was opened in the late 1850s. The road begins to curve left but you turn right between two bungalows into a field. Go through a gateway and keep ahead to go through another now coming closer to the old trackbed.

Walk ahead, virtually alongside the old railway, to a stile which you cross. In the next field head towards the outbuildings of Mill farm, passing through the gate and in front of the farmhouse as the track curves around to the right beneath the steep wooded slope towards the river. The owners of the farm in the last century must have been almost frightened out of their wits by steam trains using the nearby line, iron monsters scaring the cattle and shattering a tranquillity that had existed for centuries. Go slightly left through a gateway and head across the field to a stile which brings you onto a lane.

Tramway

Go right and walk along the delightful lane by cottages and through Lyonshall wood. This was once the route of an old tramway between Kington and Eardisley, an extension of a route from Brecon which was built in the 1820s to carry material to and from the then Kington iron foundry and also rock from Burlingjobb quarry. You come to a junction at the rise of a hill. Go left and around the corner the lane brings you to the main A44 road.

Lyonshall Church

Turn left and then after the nursery left again along a track between hedges. Go through the barred gate into a field. Head slightly right here to the tapering corner where you go through another barred gate before turning right through a small gate and then left over a stile. Head slightly right across this field to another stile and a few paces after go left through an iron gate before the vicarage. This brings you to the entrance of Lyonshall church and the castle site beyond. The church of St. Michael dates from the thirteenth century but was restored in the last century. The castle earthworks and a little stonework is all that remains of a formidable fortress probably built by the de Lacy family in the later part of the eleventh century.

If not walking into the main part of the village, leave the church and cross thee main road to walk down a track signed to Lynhales. If stopping at Lyonshall, cross the road, turn left to pass the old Weymouth Arms and then right into the village, a short walk along the Hereford road. Pass the old railway station building on high and then come to The Royal George public house, the only survivor out of eight so they say. Turn right and when the road curves left by the village stores keep ahead. Pass the buttresses of the old railway line and turn right opposite the old lodge along a wooded track to another gate which you go through. Turn right to another and then keep ahead along the field's edge until you reach a stile on the right which is crossed. Cut slightly right across the field to join the bridleway to Lynhales. Turn left here.

This lanes comes to a junction before a pool. Take the left fork and within a very short distance the less obvious left fork again. This soon brings you to a junction where you' make a right turning to pass à house and shortly Lynhales farm. Go through the gate by the house and then left through another gate into a large field. Follow the hedge to the field corner, go through the barred gate and head slightly left to a barred gate to the left of farm buildings.

Rodds Wood

Go through the gate and then another immediately to your right. Proceed across this rougher pasture towards Green cottages in the distance, cross the stile in the trough and cut across left to the stile leading into the lane to the right of the cottages. Go through the barred gate ahead and the path is slightly right towards Rodds wood, crossing the farm track and then keeping in the same direction to another stile. Cross this to enter the wood, the summit of the walk and pause at the stile on the other side as the view of Kington and The Radnor Forest beyond is precious. The location of Kington as a gap town between Hergest Ridge and Bradnor Hill, lying on the banks of Back Brook and the River Arrow, is very clear from this point.

The walking is now easy, with a gentle descent to Kington through quiet farming country. Drop down to the corner of the field ahead, cross the stile and make your way to the next one along a line of trees. Once over go slightly left aiming for a stile just to the left of the bottom left corner. Cross it and cut the corner of the next field before following the hedge on the right to another stile which you cross. Keep ahead again through a gap and another pasture to a stile. Go over this and bear left along the hedge to a footbridge and then ahead to a gate and the main A4111 road.

Cross here and beyond the pens turn right down the old Eardisley road, turn left at the bottom and walk up Bridge street into Kington town.

14. KINNERSLEY

A short walk in a flatter part of the county, from the church to the old station inn, crossing the trackbed of the Hereford to Brecon railway. Ideal for an afternoon or morning outing to visit Kinnersley, Almeley and Eardisley.

Distance: 2 miles

How To Get There:

By Bus: There is a very limited service to Kinnersley, the nearest regular bus being to Letton, $2^1/_2$ miles away.

By Car: Take the A438 road towards Hay-on-Wye and turn right at Letton not far after The Swan Inn. Follow this to the A4112, turn right and soon the church is on the right. There is limited parking by Kinnersley church.

Refreshment: The Kinnersley Arms or The Swan at Letton which keeps a good pint of beer and is usually open all day serving teas and refreshments as well as alcohol. The Kinnersley Arms was built for the coming of the railway in the mid-nineteenth century. It was known originally as the Railway Hotel, but was subsequently renamed the 'Belle Vue' Hotel, according to the locals because the then owner came from Belle Vue in Manchester. The deeds, however, suggest that he really came from Middlesex! This family run pub, with hosts Gary and Jay Fitzgerald, serves draught Bass and traditional Banks's beers. It also has a wide-ranging menu, and has become very popular in recent years.

Nearest Tourist Information: St. Owen Street, Hereford HR1 2PJ. Tel: (0432) 268430

The Elizabethan house, Kinnersley castle, standing behind the church occupies a site of a much earlier fortress built by the Kinnersley family. This passed to the de la Bere family, people of considerable character as the following yarn illustrates. In the late 1400s Kinnersley castle was the scene of intrigue when the Duke of Buckinghamshire, who hailed from

Weobley, had been caught plotting the king's downfall. Under the circumstances, he left his children with the de la Beres for safety at Kinnersley castle. More than once, the king's spies came looking for the children but the lady of the house managed to smuggle them to nearby secret haunts and even dressed the son as a girl to avoid detection. Through these cunning deeds the children survived to see adulthood. Things appear to have been less frenetic in years after this period.

The church has an unusual saddleback roofed tower which somehow seems to blend delightfully with the castle in the background. Inside there are many monuments of note including kneeling figures and sculptures.

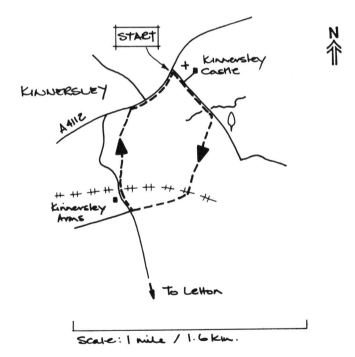

Start the walk from the entrance to Kinnersley churchyard. Turn left and follow the tarmac lane as it dips gently to a drainage ditch. Look for a stile in the hedge on the right. Go over it and cross the sleeper bridge across another drainage ditch. Cut across to the corner of the field nearest to you and then keep ahead with the hedge to your left.

Brecon Line

Go through the gate and onwards to the old railway line still protected by two kissing gates. This was the line from Hereford to Three Cocks Junction and Brecon which closed to passenger trains in the early 1960s and not longer after the weekly freight to Eardisley ceased. Like the Hereford to Gloucester line this trackbed would make a superb cycleway, allowing a traffic free route into the Herefordshire countryside. An organisation called Sustrans has been working on similar schemes throughout the country turning old railway lines into cycle routes. Could it happen in Herefordshire?

Kinnersley Arms

Leave the old railway behind. Walk along the edge of the wood to a gap in the hedge and then turn right along a hedge which soon curves away right. Head to the left of the white building, The Kinnersley Arms, and as you come nearer to the hedge you will see the remains of an old stile leading onto the road at a junction. Turn right to the inn and, if not calling in, continue over the bridge by the remains of the old railway station, no longer a pretty sight for it is full of vehicles and scrap.

Go right through the barred gate after the bridge and bear slightly left, aiming eventually for the half timbered house on the right in the distance. Cross a stile and walk a short field to cross another. Keep ahead along the hedge until it drops away and head slightly right across the field to exit at a small gate onto the main road.

Turn right to return to the church. There's a pavement on the other side of the road. Notice the spelling of Leominster on the old milepost, pronounced 'Lemster'.

15. LLANGROVE

A walk between two south Herefordshire villages across fields and with climbs in places. Good views of Llangarron in the valley of the Garron brook. The walk passes a cycle hire holiday company for those who fancy a ride through the quieter lanes of the county.

Distance: 5 miles

Map: Pathfinder Sheets 1064 Ross-on-Wye (West) and 1087 Monmouth

How To Get There:

By Bus: There is a very limited service throughout the week although the Ross Dial-a-Ride service on Tuesdays allows three hours to complete the walk which is fine.

By Car: Travel to Whitchurch on the A40(T) from Ross-on-Wye taking care to exit into the village and turn right by The Crown for Llangrove or the A49 south from Hereford, then the A4137 taking a right turn at the second junction after The New Inn at St. Owens Cross (a fine pub, dating from the early 1700s, serving Smiles' beer from Bristol). There is limited car parking on the roads in the village particularly near to the village hall.

Refreshment: The Royal Arms, a friendly pub selling draught beers and food. Village Store.

Nearest Tourist Information: 20 Broad Street, Ross-on-Wye HR9 7EA. Tel: (0989) 62768

Start from the entrance gates of Llangrove school at a fork in the road and by the garage and welding business. Notice the old village tap dating from the last century. Before this time well water would have the order of the day in such an isolated village situated on high ground. In many respects Llangrove is still very self sufficient as a working rather than dormitory community, hence the survival of the school, garage, shop and pub.

Evidently, the village used to be called Long Grove in earlier centuries but has been referred to as Llangrove for the past three to four hundred years, so it is not likely to revert to its old label. It would be interesting to have a local referendum to find out which is preferred by the residents!

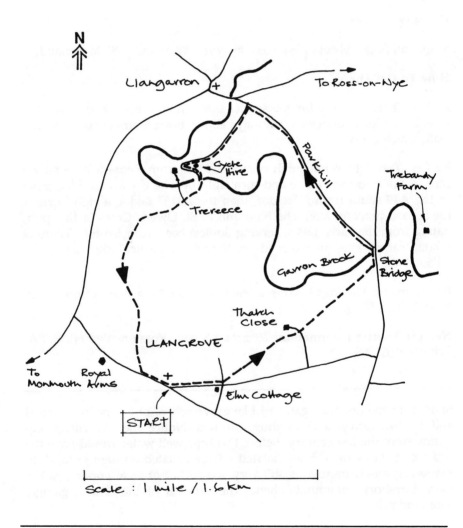

Courts

Within a short distance you come to a cross roads where the path leads through a kissing gate on the left and down a field, slightly right to meet a hedge. Go left along it towards a large house, Thatch Close, partly hidden by trees. Cross the stile into the next field and walk to the right of and beyond the house to come across a stile over the iron railings and onto the drive. Go through the gap in the hedge, which looks more akin to an entrance to Narnia, cross the stile and begin to walk down the field with the hedge to your left. There are good views across the valley and to Trebandy farm ahead. The area has several traditional farmhouses and courts with Langstone court and Ruxton court farm nearby. Follow through a succession of fields in this way until a stile exits by way of steps to a tarmac road at Stone Bridge.

St. Deinst

Go over the bridge and turn left to climb up a lane known as Parkmill and then down towards Llangarron. Follow this into the village if you wish to visit the church of St. Deinst. This has an unusual dedication to a Celtic saint and is in a lovely spot. There's no pub in the village but a good shop, an antiques and second hand shop, and a chain saw specialist! Nevertheless, it is well worth the detour on your route.

Otherwise, turn left as you approach the village after a group of houses on the right and follow this lane for a little over a quarter of a mile. It begins to drop by a superbly restored house, the base for Pedal Away cycles (098984) 357 who offer short break and longer cycling packages. The beauty of the scheme is the back up facilities if you need it miles away from base.

The lane curves left to Trereece by buildings nestled alongside the Garron brook which looks peaceful now but can become something of a torrent after really heavy rain. Go over the bridge and before the farm turn right up an old lane, eroded by the streams that appear in winter but dry at most times. As this track curves right keep ahead to cross a stile into the field.

Walk alongside the hedge to your left to cross another stile and keep company with this next section of hedge until reaching a stile beyond a gap. Cross it and follow the hedge up to the corner to meet another path. Turn left and follow the hedge on the right until it indents right. Keep ahead to cross a stile and after twenty paces or so in this next field summon the energy to climb up the bank heading slightly right to the corner of a fence. Follow this up to wooden rails by a gate and then head slightly left to exit onto a lane at a barred gate between a cottage and new building.

This leads to a tarmac lane. Go left for the school or right for The Royal.

Victorian Tap, Llangrove

16. LONGTOWN

Walking through sheep farming country in the foothills of the Black Mountains. There is one major climb out of Longtown but the path is clear if not marked for most of the route.

Distance: 3 to 4 miles

Map: Pathfinder Sheet 1063 Longtown and Pandy

How To Get There:

By Bus: Longtown has a very limited bus service mainly to serve the needs of schoolchildren. However, there is a superb market day bus service between Hereford and Abergavenny on Tuesday mornings which provides a ride up the Dulas valley to Longtown with a return journey mid afternoon. This is ideal timing for the walk allowing a lunch stop in Longtown.

By Car: Turn off the A465 Hereford to Abergavenny road at The Pandy Inn, signed to Longtown. There is a limited amount of car parking on the Hay road past the Crown Inn and Post Office on the way up to the castle ruins.

Refreshment: The Crown at Longtown and The Cornewell Arms at Clodock. While in the area try The Bridge at Michaelchurch Escley which serves a couple of draught beers, good food and has a camping ground. The Post Office in Longtown sells local produce including spring water from a local farm.

Nearest Tourist Information: Swan Meadow, Abergavenny, Gwent, NP7 5HH. Tel: (0873) 77588.

Longtown is as straddled as the name suggests with the remains of an early Norman castle at the top end of the village and the pub at the other end. The castle was built by the de Lacys and the remaining stonework includes an early round keep. For centuries the castle was the focal part of the village with the church and old square nearby. The

Outdoor Centre across the road was at one time a pub and also where the Court leet met to sort out petty misdemeanours. Thus, it eventually became known as the Court House.

The village is the base for schoolchildren and other outdoor groups setting off into the Black Mountains by way of the Olchon valley. The weather can get very rough on the mountains and every year the mountain rescue team based here is called out to deal with emergencies. One yarn is that an old farmer roams the hills guiding lost walkers to

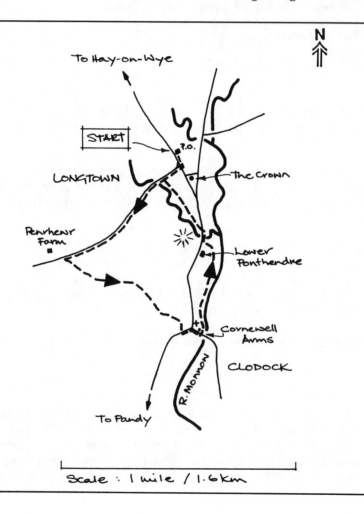

N

To Hay-on-Wye

START

P.O.

LONGTOWN

The Crown

Penrhewr Farm

Lower Ponthendre

Cornewell Arms

CLODOCK

R. MONNOW

To Pandy

Scale : 1 mile / 1.6 km

safety and then disappears into the hillside but your chances of meeting him on this lower level walk are slim.

River Monnow

Start from Longtown Post Office and stores, a place which not only sells stamps and newspapers but also local produce such as honey, eggs and Herefordshire spring water. Turn right at the triangular junction and follow the tarmac lane, first to cross the clear running River Monnow then to climb up towards the Black Mountains. There are exceptional views over gateways of the Olchon valley to your right, a most secluded part of Herefordshire providing a living for scattered hill farms.

After approximately one quarter of a mile Penrhewr farm comes into view. You will see a wide concrete drive on the right and at this point turn left to climb above the lane and through a gateway. Head slightly left across the field to a stile. Maintain a similar course in the next field to cross fencing by a stone. The views across the Monnow valley and toward Pandy are superb here.

Turn left and go through the right hand barred gate then turn right to follow the field's edge to the corner and then left to a gateway which you go through. A glance at the Pathfinder shows the path running down the opposite side of this hedge but as the way looks to have been blocked for years this is your nearest alternative, although the original route might be re-opened by the time you walk it. Look for the stile on the left, walk down to the small stream and then up to the meadow adjacent to the graveyard. Go slightly right across this field to exit onto a tarmac lane.

Clodock

Turn left and at the junction by Clodock church, bear right to pass the Cornewell Arms. Just before the bridge over the River Monnow, go left to pass by cottages and through the churchyard. Pause here to view this simple mediaeval church dedicated to St Clodock (originally Clydawg), the only one in the country. Thereby hangs a tale for Clydawg was the son of the King of Ewyas an upstanding, chaste young Christian man. Clydwag was to be married to a local noblewoman but instead met a bloody death at the hands of a rival suitor (and a bad company of friends). Returning homewards with the dead body, the animals pulling the cart stopped and refused to cross the river at this very spot. All concerned took this to mean that God wished this to be his burial place and that it should be a holy site so the church was built here at Clodock.

Note the stone stile, sadly an old gravestone. Keep ahead through narrow fields with the Monnow to the right, through a gateway and then crossing a stile. In the next field walk along river's edge at first but then bear slightly left to go through a barred gate. Cross a stile and walk through the paddock behind Lower Ponthendre farm to a stone stile. Cross this and follow the hedge on the left to cross two stiles close together and finally onto the road.

Turn right, walk over the bridge and then go left over a stone stile. After a short while, leave the river bank towards the corner of a hedge ahead. Look for the stile on the right, cross it and turn left to walk a short section to cross another stile. Proceed ahead to pass through the gap and cross another stile. Go through the gate onto the tarmac road and turn right to retrace you steps into Longtown.

17. LUGWARDINE

Easy walking around this large village near to Hereford along a low ridge which offers unusual views of Hereford city. Nearby is the Lugg Meadows a riverside stretch of land, of considerable scientific interest and threatened by a relief road.

Distance: 3 miles

Map: Pathfinder sheet 1017 Hereford (North)

How To Get There:

By Bus: There is a bus on Monday to Saturday from Hereford. Ask for Lugwardine church.

By Car: Take the A438 road from Hereford to Lugwardine. There is limited parking in the village near before the church.

Refreshment: The Crown and Anchor inn serving Whitbread beers

Nearest Tourist Information: St. Owen Street, Hereford HR1 2PJ. Tel: (0432) 268430

The road from Hereford crosses the Lugg meadows, an ancient strip of land divided among commoners for grazing their animals on these fertile flood plains. To the walker it simply looks a flat expanse with a path between Lugg mill in the north and the Lugg bridge at Lugwardine. To the naturalist the unusual cultivation pattern has led to a rich haven for wildlife, birds and butterflies. This is threatened by the proposed ring road which will disturb the site forever. A classic example of conflict between conservation and economic development, although some have doubts that if a road is built that it will do the job.

Lugwardine is a large village surprisingly not much influenced by the close proximity of Hereford and neighbouring village Bartestree. If there is a focal point, it is the church set back from the main road with a commanding view over the Lugg valley. It dates back to the thirteenth century and has been skilfully restored over the centuries.

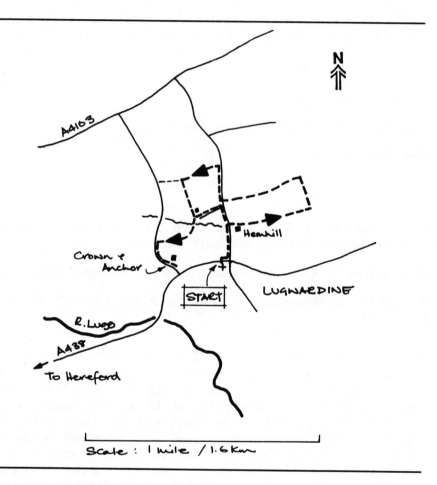

Sweet Briar

Start the walk at Lugwardine church. Cross the road, turn right and then first left walking along a pleasant back lane by old cottages two of which are known as Rose and Sweet Briar. They were at one time the base of a local brick company long since gone but which supplied rich red bricks from nearby clays to builders of the area. Look for a renovated farm and extraordinarily high garden hedge on your right, the kind of hedge which defies the largest of kicked footballs. Just by this house turn right over a stile and walk along the field's edge to join a track. Keep ahead with the hedge to your left. The houses in the distance belong to neighbouring Bartestree village. Look back over Lugwardine church to The Woolhopes.

The pathfinder map indicates that the path is through the gap on the left and following the field edge right and then left. Most locals, however, have trodden a well worn path on the other side of the hedge. Thus, cross the stile by the gate and turn left. At the spinney turn left and cross the stile into a field with the hedge on your right.

Pyon Hill

Keep ahead with the hedge now to your left, with views of Dinmore and Wormsley with the pinnacle of Pyon hill in the middle: a mysterious hill which looks as if it belongs to the page of a fairy tale book. Cross the next stile and drop down a track to a drive and then onto a tarmac lane. Go right here and walk along the road into the plain. Within a short distance, cross a stile on the left opposite a barred gate. Head slightly left and cross a stile and ahead again to cross another stile into a small enclosure. Turn left and follow the hedge to yet another stile and into an old orchard with standard trees.

Keep ahead to join a lane by a half timbered cottage, go through the gate ahead onto the green and walk towards the little bridge but then there's a choice of routes. You can either turn left along the well worn path towards several half-timbered cottages. Turn right onto the lane and at the next major junction turn right again to retrace steps back to the church.

On the other hand cross the bridge and exit in the corner of the field. Keep ahead along a well worn path through two small fields to a lane and then turn left to pass, almost by chance, the Crown and Anchor public house.

18. MATHON

A short walk around this quiet village in the shoulder hills of The Malverns.

Distance: 4 miles

Map: Pathfinder sheet 1018 Great Malvern

How To Get There:

By Bus: With extreme difficulty. Nearest buses at Cradley or Colwall with two mile walk.

By Car: Travel on the A4103 road between Hereford and Worcester and after Stifford's Bridge (with a pub on either side) turn next right to pass through the old village of Cradley and as signed to Mathon. There is very little car parking near to the church.

Refreshment: The Cliffe Arms, Mathon. When in the area also try the CAMRA recommended Brewers Arms at West Malvern serving Marston's beers.

Nearest Tourist Information: Winter Gardens, Grange Road, Great Malvern, WR14 3HB. Tel: (0684) 892289.

Mathon lies between gently folded hills to the west of the main flank of The Malverns. Famous for its hop culture, the 'Mathon White', although little seems to be grown now and its red sand, the village has for the most part been engaged in agriculture over the centuries. Recent conversion of old farm buildings to dwellings is evidence of a change in the village but for the most part Mathon is likely to continue as it has done so over the decades.

The church dominates the skyline of the walk and contains some splendid Norman architecture. It contains several effigies and tablets, including those of a well known local Cliffe family featured in the naming of the village pub.

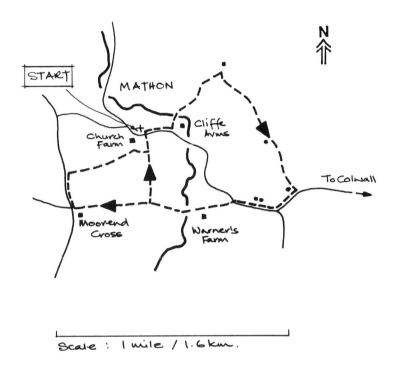

Start from the entrance to the church. Turn left and walk towards the Cliffe Arms but before reaching it look for a narrow path between hedge and fence on the left. Cross the footbridge and stile to enter an open field with a track. Turn right along the track and follow this up to the top of the field to the right of a house. Go through a gate on the right here and walk ahead with the hedge to your left. Go through the gap near to the far corner and then turn right through a barred gate. Keep ahead and pass to the left of a cottage. Follow the track to a tarmac lane where you turn right.

Village Hall

Follow this lane past houses and Mathon village hall. Take care beyond here as the road narrows to a blind bend. Cross over before the corner and walk ahead by an old sand pit along a path signed to Moorend

Cross. The path passes to the right of Warner's farm and to a stile by a gate. Cross it and turn left to the stream where you cross a footbridge, turn right and head across the field to a stile in the hedge corner.

In the next field keep ahead with the hedge to your left. Cross the stile onto the track. For a shorter walk go right along this track back to the church. For those who fancy another mile, turn left to cross another stile and then right. Keep ahead with the hedge to your right, cross a stile in the corner and walk ahead once again to join a track alongside a farm. At the road turn right and keep ahead. As the lane winds down to a corner go over the stile on the right by a barred gate and turn right to head along the right hand side of the field towards Mathon church and village.

Sundial on old cross, Cradley church

Go through the gateway and then ahead but to the right of the buildings. Cross the next stile and head slightly right across the field to another stile. Once over, turn left down the track to return to Mathon church. The Cliffe Arms is near to hand, a pub which has retained a bar and lounge, and has seats outside. Thankfully, some things never change, or at least only gradually.

When in the area take time to visit the nearby village of Cradley with its delightful church and historic buildings.

19. MORDIFORD

A great walk through beautiful countryside varying from grazing pastures to coniferous woodland. The Woolhope Dome is a place for walkers and this circular with a few climbs could not be a better introduction.

Distance: 7 miles

Map: Pathfinder sheet 1040 Hereford (South)

How To Get There:

By Bus: There is a Monday to Saturday service from Hereford to Mordiford. Ask for The Moon.

By Car: Travel on the B4224 road to Mordiford. There is a limited amount of on street parking in the village but please park considerately.

Refreshment: The Moon at Mordiford selling Whitbread beers and The Yew Tree at Priors Frome, a lively pub serving a choice of real ales and food. CAMRA recommended. There is also a shop in Mordiford.

Nearest Tourist Information Centre: St. Owen Street, Hereford HR1 2PJ. Tel: (0432) 268430

Everyone has heard about the Mordiford dragon, so take care on this walk. A story is told that near the banks of the Pentaloe Brook (which you'll meet in about 5 miles) lived a fussy old dragon, fussy because he loved eating humans instead of animals. As the villagers realised that humans were soon to be scarce, they press ganged a condemned convict into slaying the dragon – which he did. He hid in a barrel and when the dragon came for his slurp the criminal shot the dragon between the eyes but unfortunately didn't survive to tell the tale himself for the dragon breathed heavy fumes over him before expiring.

Mordiford Bridge

On a more serious note Mordiford was quite a busy milling centre. A mill to your right, near The Moon, is currently being restored. A fair amount of transhipment of goods from the river took place and also wood gathered for tanning most probably at Fownhope. Research has shown that the River Lugg was busier with boats than previously

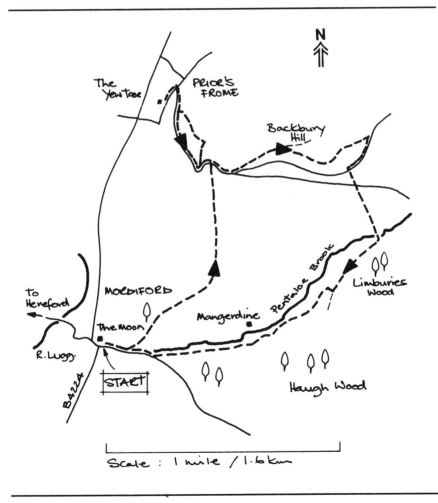

estimated. It is now certain that there were locks on the river as far upstream as Leominster including one near the magnificent Mordiford bridge, the first to be officially recorded by Herefordshire County Council.

The church stands in a lovely setting and is well worth a visit. Dating mainly from the thirteenth century, it has interesting monuments and effigies.

Start the walk at Woolhope turning in Mordiford by The Moon public house. Walk a short distance along the road and turn first left up a steep track past cottages. The track is signed as 'The Mordiford Loop Walk' on the longest wooden sign to be seen for a good few miles around. This is part of The Wye Valley walk and the path to Priors Frome has been improved and well waymarked.

Not far up the track, look for steps up left into the wood which then turn right to climb to a stile which you cross. Keep ahead to cross another stile and ahead to cross another with a small wood now to your left. Go through the silage pit to cross two stiles in succession and simply keep ahead across the fields along this lovely ridge offering views to Hereford and beyond or to the Woolhope Dome. The path eventually exits into a narrow wood by way of a stile and then turns right to join a tarmac road.

The Yew Tree

For a half mile detour to Priors Frome, turn left and walk down the road – but be vigilant for a stile at the top of the bend. If you find this too awkward try the gateway on the other side of the white railings. Walk down the valley by a barn and exit by the farm onto the lane once again. Otherwise, simply follow the lane down to this point continuing to the junction where you turn left for The Yew Tree. Nearby is Sufton Court which is set in gardens set out by famous landscape gardener and designer Humphry Repton. Much of it can be seen from the Mordiford to Priors Frome road.

Backbury Hill

Retrace steps back up the hill and just over the brow turn left along a bridleway. The track soon forks beneath Backbury hill. Some writers say that this is where Ethelbert, King of Mercia set camp before his final battle with Offa at Sutton Walls in the latter part of the eight century. Take the lower fork and follow this gently downwards at first then a little steeper until it joins another track and curves down to a lane by a house. Turn right and within a short distance look for a stile on the left after a house and small orchard. It is almost opposite a hidden cottage on the other side of the track. Cross the stile and walk down the field to exit at a stile beneath an oak tree. This area is known as Clouds and just along the road is the hamlet of Checkley, at one time a favourite haunt for young geologists arriving on the twice weekly Red and White bus in search for brachiopod and trilobite fossils embedded in the limestone rock strata nearby.

Once on the road go left and then right along a track, across the bridge and Limburies wood. Just beyond, the path leads off to the right alongside the fence and then comes to a stile which you cross. Keep ahead in the field at first but then cut up left to a stile leading into the extremity of Haugh wood. The path curves left up a bank to meet a U-bend of a forestry track. Take the lower fork and continue along it until it approaches a meadow and the Pentaloe Brook (Watch out for dragons).

The main track bends right but you keep ahead. This climbs a little and then be on the look out for a path between the tall conifers which leads down to a gate and into a meadow with a derelict cottage on the right. Join the track and turn left. The path, however, leaves the track as it curves away left and heads across the field slightly right to exit by the bungalows. Go between garden fences to the road and turn right. It is possible also to return alongside the brook if you prefer.

20. MORTIMER'S CROSS

A short walk to the village of Lucton returning through fields alongside the River Lugg. Pleasant walking country with few climbs

Distance: 3 miles

Map: Pathfinder Sheet 972 Mortimers Cross and Tenbury Wells.

How To Get There:

By Bus: There is a limited service from Leominster and a college days only bus from Hereford to Mortimer's Cross. Contact Teme Valley Motors for details on (054 73) 223

By Car: Travel on the A4110 road from Hereford to Knighton road. There is limited parking near to the crossroads

Refreshment: Mortimers's Cross inn with an electrifying bar and a lounge with a fair number of pictures reflecting an aircraft theme. The pub is close to Shobdon airport so it is not too surprising. The pub serves real ales as well as snacks and meals. It is a jolly place for a break.

Nearest Tourist Information: 6 School Lane, Leominster, HR6 8AA. Tel: (0568) 6460.

What a lonely place this must have been after the battle of Mortimer's Cross in 1461 with so many dead in such a brief encounter. How different battle would have been in those mediæval times. No deadly missile weapons programmed with utmost precision to devastate a target hundred of miles away, no technically sophisticated ground weaponry.

The Battle

It was an important battle in The War of the Roses between Yorkists and Lancastrians. It is chronicled that, on the morning of the engagement three suns were seen in the sky. Edward Mortimer leading the Yorkists camp, took as an omen of fortune spreading the word to his troops to stir their courage in the fight to come. Succeed he did for the Lancastrians were defeated, hunted down and their leaders killed publicly in Hereford. Edward then proceeded to London to become King Edward IV. It looks so peaceful now, as if there could never have been a wanton shedding of life on these gentle slopes surrounding the Lugg.

A monument dating from 1799 commemorates the battle and stands beside the nearby Monument Inn on the outskirts of Kingsland:

This pedestal is erected to perpetuate the Memory of an obstinate, bloody and decisive battle fought near this Spot in the Civil Wars between the ambitious Houses of York and Lancaster on the 2nd day of February 1460, between the Forces of Edward Mortimer, Earl of March (afterwards Edward the Fourth) on the side of York and those of Henry the Sixth on the side of Lancaster. The King's Troops were commanded by Jasper, The Earl of Pembroke. Edward commanded his own in Person and was victorious. The slaughter was great on both sides – four Thousands being left dead on the Field and many Welsh Persons of the first distinction were taken Prisoners among whom Owen Tudor (Great Grandfather of Henry the Eight and a descendant of the illustrious Cadwallader), who was afterwards beheaded at Hereford. This was the decisive Battle which fixed Edward the Fourth on the Throne of England, who was proclaimed King in London on the fifth of March following.

Erected by Subscription In the year 1799

The monument cites the date of the battle as 1460 but historians agree that the stonemason was a year out in his calculations but otherwise he did well to get the story chiselled out on such stone with such accuracy.

Start the walk from Mortimers Cross. Turn left to walk along the edge of the B4362 road towards Ludlow, crossing the road and the bridge. To the left is Lucton mill, an eighteenth century water mill used to make paper then to grind corn. It evidently worked until the Second World war and fell into disuse, but has since been restored. The mill is open from

Stone milepost, Mortimer's Cross

April to September on two or three days a week and is occasionally set
to work again to crush fodder for animals.

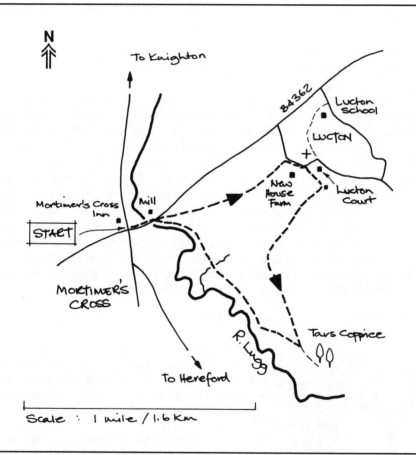

N

To Knighton

B4362

Lucton
School

LUCTON

+

New
House
Farm

Lucton
Court

Mortimer's Cross
Inn

Mill

START

MORTIMER'S
CROSS

Taws Coppice

R. Lugg

To Hereford

Scale : 1 mile / 1.6 Km

Lucton

Just beyond the bridge over the River Lugg, cross the stile on the right
and then bear slightly left up the field to go through a gate into the next
field. Keep ahead and Lucton school appears in the distance, a good
looking building dating from the early eighteenth century, the school

having been established by John Pierrepont in 1708 and still going strong nearly two hundred years later.

Cross the stile adjacent to the gate and walk straight ahead once again to cross another stile. Pass a pole as the path leads to a further gate and track which brings you onto a tarmac road in the village by New House farm. Go right and follow the lane past the old barns and then, after a modern house and before the half timbered Lucton Court, dating mainly from the sixteenth and seventeenth centuries, turn right to pass through two gateways and ahead through a narrow pasture.

Should you wish to look at Lucton church walk past Lucton court and turn left at the junction. There is a walk from the rear of the church yard through to the school and then turning right back along the lane to Lucton Hall where another field path returns back to the road junction where you previously turned left. It is a pretty church dating mainly from 1850 which includes a commemorative tablet to the school's founder dating from 1711.

For those not considering the extension the path through the narrow pasture meets a wide track. This is not the right of way shown on the pathfinder, which should cut right across a field to meet this track. Hopefully, this path will be reopened. Turn right and follow it until it gives out into a field. Once again the right of way shown on the pathfinder sheet is not feasible, i.e. cutting slightly left across the field but this could well be reinstated in future. In the meantime, use the track alongside the hedge on the right through gates and up to the field corner but as it curves right to join the higher ground, keep ahead along the fence, now on your right, until you reach a gate. Go through it and climb the bank up to a gateway on your left. There are views across the Lugg valley to Kingsland from here as you head slightly right across the field to the right of a wood to a gate. Do not go through it.

Islands

Meet another path here. Turn around with the gate behind you and head back across the field but slightly left to a barred gate. Once over, go slightly left towards the river bank, through another gateway and then proceed ahead between the bluff on your right and the river to your left: a superb stretch with meanderings and islands which make it a haven for wildlife with a liking for shallow waters as well as for those who enjoy fishing.

The field opens up beyond the bluff but keep ahead, thus moving away from the river, to a stile and footbridge over a drainage channel. Cross both and maintain a course ahead along a gentle rise above the river banks, to a gate and back to the stile by the B4362. Turn left to retrace your steps with time for a visit to the mill or a touch of refreshment at The Mortimer's Cross inn.

21. MUCH BIRCH

Easy walking over clear paths with one or two climbs. Not a part of the county that is walked very much except by locals but the valley of the Wriggle brook a trickle of a stream, is a quiet retreat between Little and Much Birch.

Distance: 5 miles

Map: Pathfinder Sheet 1040 Hereford (South) & Area

How To Get There:

By Bus: There is a daily service, 38, between Hereford and Ross-on-Wye which serves Much Birch including Sunday afternoons.

By Car: Travel on the main A49 to Much Birch. There is a little parking by The Axe and Cleaver public house or alternatively near to Much Birch church, half a mile closer to Hereford. Be careful as the stretch of road in Much Birch encourages drivers to pass at great speed.

Refreshment: The Axe and Cleaver is a friendly public house which serves draught Whitbread beers, Marston's Pedigree and Charrington's IPA and offers a selection of bar and restaurant meals. The Castle, also known sometimes as The Pendant, in Little Birch offers a range of draught beers and snacks. There is a stores and post office in Kingsthorne.

Nearest Tourist Information: St Owen St. Hereford, HR1 2JP. Tel: (0432) 268430

Much Birch does not have one centre but is spread in and around the main A49 road. With traffic moving so fast, people tend not to linger by the roadside. There is a most interesting old part around the church which dates from mediaeval times but was mainly restored in the late 1830s.

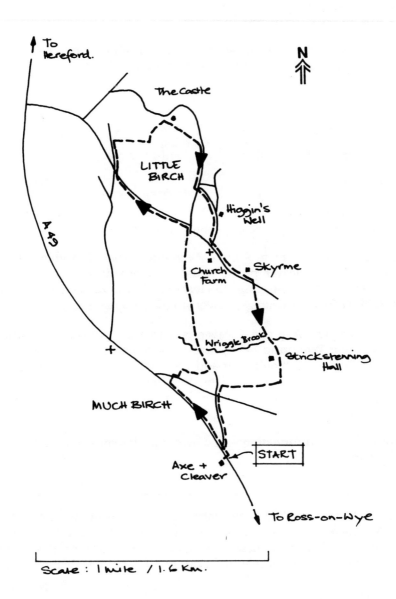

To Hereford.

N

The Castle

LITTLE BIRCH

A49

Higgin's Well

Church Farm

Skyrme

Wriggle Brook

Strickstenning Hall

MUCH BIRCH

START

Axe + Cleaver

To Ross-on-Wye

Scale : 1 mile / 1.6 Km.

Hay Carts

Start from the Axe and Cleaver public house by crossing the road and walking on the pavement up a gentle hill to a path just beyond a bus lay-by opposite the old Much Birch stores. This little link path crosses a lane, Hollybush lane, over two stiles by an old barn and into a field where you head slightly right down the field to a gap between hedges. Follow the hedge on the right to another stile. Cross this and drop down to a sunken lane, no doubt full of hay carts earlier in the century and now full of nettles so pick your way through carefully. Go left down to cross a footbridge and to a stile which leads into a large field. Go right.

Within a few paces, however, bear slightly right to join the old sunken lane once again, a haven for wildlife and which sometimes becomes a stream after wet weather.

Go through the barred gates and keep ahead along a green lane to meet the corner of a tarmac road. Go left and at the next junction left again. Follow this road to a junction where you bear right uphill along a track. Shortly look for a stile on the right which you cross. Follow the hedge on the left to cross another stile. Keep ahead with the hedge to your left to a stile by a gate near to a house. Walk along the lane and at Back House as the lane bends left go over a stile on the right . Go through the enclosure to cross a stile ahead and exit onto a lane.

Higgin's Well

The Castle public house, a very local pub tucked away in this part of Little Birch, is ahead but if not calling in, turn right down a track to a lower road. Turn right here and as the lane begins to descend more steeply turn second left down a track by houses. This becomes rougher as it drops to Higgin's Well, named after a grumpy old farmer who at first resented local folk using the water supply but, after receiving a watery omen, was more than pleased to allow both human and beast to the well. It was restored by public goodwill and money to commemorate the Diamond Jubilee of Queen Victoria's reign in 1897. Pass to the right of it and then walk slightly right up the hill to a tarmac road once again.

Bear left and walk past the fine church of Little Birch restored by well known church architect Chick in the last century but thought to have

very early origins.   It is one of the quietest spots in Herefordshire.
Continue along the lane which now becomes a rougher track. Pass a
farm on the left and then look for a stile on the right as the track begins
to descend more steeply. Cross the stile and walk around the pond to
the hedge on the left which you follow into the valley and Wriggle
Brook.

Higgin's Well

Go over a sleeper bridge, stile and old gate and walk up the field with Strickstenning hall to the right, a fine looking building in landscaped ground. Your path curves slightly left around the perimeter fence and buildings but then comes closer to the hedge on the right again as you climb the bank to a stile in the top right hand corner. Cross this and another stile on the right. Walk along this path to cross another stile and then through another field to cross another stile leading into a lane.

Turn left and follow this to a crossroads. Keep ahead to the Axe and Cleaver or turn right to return to Much Birch church.

22. ORLETON

Easy walking between Orleton and Eye in a gentle valley. The route includes a chance to see the remains of The Stourport, Leominster and Kington canal, Eye Manor and church and Berrington Park.

Distance: 8 miles

Map: Pathfinder sheet 972 Tenbury Wells and Mortimers Cross

How To Get There:

By Bus: Travel on the daily (including Sundays) 292 service from Hereford to Leominster and Ludlow.

By Car: Orleton is on the B4361 road between Leominster and Ludlow

The village is signed to the right by Orleton Fruit farm or The Maidenhead pub. There is limited on street parking in the village.

Refreshment: The Boot which has a relaxed atmosphere, good beer and a restaurant area. There is a small detached half timbered building in the car park which is centuries old. There is also a village post office and stores nearby.

Nearest Tourist Information: 6 School Lane, Leominster HR6 8AA. Tel: (0568) 6460

Orleton is a large village by Herefordshire standards and was something of a cattle market for local farmers in past centuries. Luston, a few miles down the road, similarly specialised in sheep for The Balance Inn was known for the grading and weighing of wool. Orleton has several half-timbered houses, especially in Orleton Court.

The village was home to a rather maligned Bishop, Adam de Orleton, who became involved in intrigue against the throne, conniving with Roger Mortimer of Wigmore fame, to assassinate Edward II. Adam never returned to his native village.

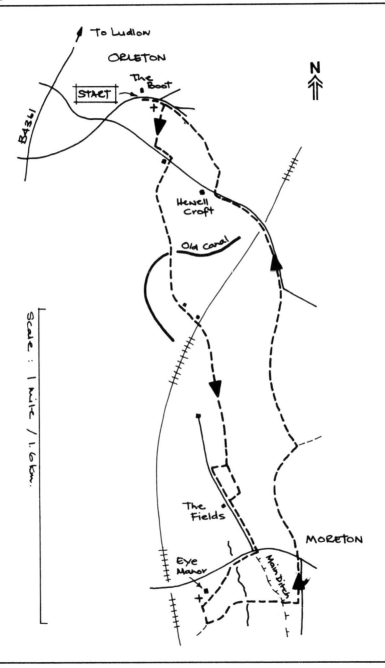

To Ludlow

ORLETON

The Boot

START

B4361

Hewell Croft

Old Canal

N

Scale : 1 mile / 1.6 km.

The Fields

MORETON

Eye Manor

Main Ditch

Start the walk from The Boot Inn. Turn left and follow the road to the junction by the old vicarage, now a residential home for the elderly. Take the right fork and then go right up steps into the churchyard. The church of Saint George dates from Norman times and has several distinctive features of note such as the font, chests and pulpit.

Just beyond it turn left and walk between graves to cross a stile into a field. There's one old story that Orleton church yard is so packed because they believed that Orleton was going to be the place where Resurrection day begins. Pull the other one, you might be saying but the churchyard does look rather packed.

Leominster Canal

Turn right and head across the field to a stile exiting into a lane. Turn left and then beyond the half timbered cottage, go right over a stile into a field with a corrugated barn to your left. Head for the stile ahead which leads into an old track where you turn left. This leads to a brick bridge over an old navigation, The Stourport, Leominster and Kington navigation. Unfortunately, the canal was never completed and only a section from Leominster to Southnet wharf was constructed a distance of about 18 miles. Look at the sleeping pools of water, encroached by reeds and scrub and read this note from the Leominster Guide of 1808, an illustration of the sheer optimism for the project:

'The whole line presents a romantic and picturesque appearance, sometimes gliding quietly through a level country, at other times hanging by the sides of hills, now hiding itself underground and now rolling its waters over subjected rives; at length descending into the Severn by seventeen locks and thereby opening a communication with every part of the world. '

Class 37

In the next field your way is ahead, with a landmark of a derelict cottage slightly left in the distance. Meet the end of an old hedge mid field and walk on the far side of it to pass the remains of an old building and then cutting across to the right of the cottage. More's the pity it is not in use. It would be ideal for anyone who has a love of trains for, being right next to the line, the place shakes no doubt every time a train passes;

especially when a sturdy Class 37 engine hauls a trainload of steel from South Wales on the up line to Crewe. Cross the lines with great care for the newer 'Sprinter' passenger trains move along at a fair speed. Ironically, the launch of this railway in The Old Assembly Rooms in Ludlow was with an impressive spread including twelve pigeon pies, one large boar's head, twelve ornamental sponge cakes and eighteen moulds of jelly. This meant the death knell for the canal. One of the first acquisitions of the railway company was the Leominster canal which it choked to death within a very short time for railways did not enjoy competition.

Once across, keep ahead to join the hedge and then turn right and proceed with the hedge on your left, through a gate and then to another with a farm on your right. Go through it, turn left and then right through other gates and then keep ahead with the hedge now to your right. Cross the stile by the next gate and walk to the next gate which leads onto the end of a track. The right of way on the Pathfinder indicates that you turn left here and immediately right. Then, at a point parallel to the second farmhouse go over a stile, which is not more than a few pieces of wood. Follow the hedge down to a gate which exits onto the drive. However, some local walkers cut down the track and turn left along the tarmac drive.

Eye Manor

This leads to another road where you turn right and once over the bridge cross a stile on the left into a field with a view of Eye Manor and church. Eye Manor was built in the latter part of the seventeenth century for Ferdinando Gorges, a unlikable character who made vast fortunes in Barbados trading in sugar and slaves. The house has many fine decorations and furnishings. The church dates from earlier times with monuments dedicated to the Cornewell family and other fine features.

Head for the church where there is a gateway allowing access. Pass by the church to the bottom of the churchyard, through a small gate and then left through another gateway into the field you have just walked and set off again to a stile and footbridge opposite, bridging the water channel known functionally as Main Ditch. Turn left and at the corner right, to follow the hedge to the gap leading onto the bridleway known as Moreton Ride, unknowingly crossing the course of the old canal once again.

If you turned right here it would lead into Berrington Park, landscaped by Capability Brown. He was an imaginative landscape gardener who caused much controversy between those wishing to see natural landscapes and others who enjoy a more contrived parkland. The debate continues but his work is evident throughout the country as at the time he was a most fashionable creator of scenery. Berrington Hall was designed by Henry Holland for a wealthy landowner Thomas Harley from Brampton Bryan castle. The property is now owned by The National Trust.

However, on this occasion, we turn left to pass by houses in the hamlet of Moreton. Cross the road and keep ahead along a superb bridleway which comes to a junction. Turn left here, along a section which opens into a field and then along a track again onto a tarmac road. Turn left and walk along the road, over the railway and beyond a farm before looking right for a track opposite a recently built farm house.

Follow the track back to Orleton church and into the village.

23. PENCOMBE

Gentle stroll around Pencombe through mixed farmland with local views of the village

Distance: 2 miles

Map: Pathfinder sheet 995 Bromyard

How To Get There:

By Bus: There is a very limited bus service to Pencombe from Hereford but the Wednesday only bus is timed ideally to allow for a walk, look at the church and visit to the pub.

By Car: Take the A465 road to Stoke Hill, before Stoke Lacy where the road to Ullingswick and Pencombe is signed left. There is limited car parking in the village near to the church.

Refreshment: The Wheelwrights pub in Pencombe village serves a draught beer and snacks. This is a fine old village pub. There are also pubs in nearby Ullingswick, The Three Crowns and The Three Horseshoes in Little Cowarne. Both sell real ales and serve food.

Nearest Tourist Information: Bromyard – Council Offices, Rowberry Street, Bromyard HR7 4DX. Tel: (0885) 482341

Pencombe is hidden away amongst gently rolling hills incised by the River Lodon and its tributaries. It is firmly based in agriculture to this day with several large farmhouses dominating the landscape. Near to Pencombe, and a must for those with younger families, is Shortwood farm, which has been opened to the public by the Legge family. The beauty is that the children are encouraged to join in whether it be milking the cows, collecting hen's eggs from the most unlikely places or talking to the animals. The trail around the fields gives you a good idea about the running of this farm and a superb booklet is available to explain about Shortwood. There are special open days at certain times of the year such as cider making in the back end of autumn and Shortwood's cider is guaranteed to put hairs on your chest.

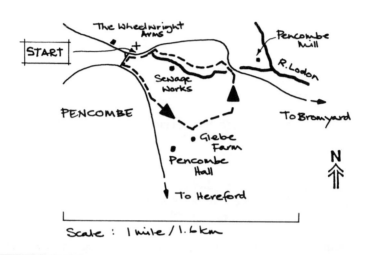

Scale : 1 mile / 1.6 km

Pencombe Hall

Start the walk from Pencombe church. Walk down the left hand side of the road triangle to the T junction and turn left. Follow the lane up the hill to a point beyond the last house and go left through the second of the barred gates. Head slightly right to cross a stile and then cut left to another stile and proceed up the field to the track to the left of Pencombe Hall, now a nursing home but at one time a Victorian hall.

Pass the modern house on the right and keep ahead to the right of the hedge. Continue along the field's edge with the hedge to your left until reaching a stile which is crossed and then the path turns left down the hill. Pencombe mill stands below to the right which evidently used to grind corn.

Cross a stile and descend to an old gate leading onto a road. Go left and left again through large gates towards the barn. As the way is shown on the map as being through the bricks and mortar, go through the gate on the right, turn left and look for the stile in the fence behind the barn. Cross it and proceed slightly right of the sewage works, nose pegged as the path leads up a track that narrows close to the brook, one of the reasons why Pencombe is situated in this hollow.

Market Day bus arriving at Pencombe

Picturesque Church

Walk to the kissing gate which leads to a road by the bungalows. The choice is yours at this point. Either go left to walk along the stream and behind houses to the small village green or turn right up the road and left back to the church and green. The picturesque church dates mainly from the nineteenth century and includes fascinating monuments, including this lament for a young explorer inscribed on a slab:

'Sacred to the memory of Richard, son of George and Elizabeth Jordan, of this parish, who led by a spirit of enterprise and a passionate love of knowledge accompanied by Mr Richard Lander in his third and last attempt to explore the interior of Africa and there fell in sacrifice to the baneful influence of the climate dying at Damuggoo, on the 21 day of Nov. 1832 in the 20th year of his age: to the inexpressible grief of his afflicted parents who in him deplore the loss of a dutiful and affectionate Son.'

The village green with war memorial and telephone kiosk looks quite serene. Around the corner of the lower road lies The Wheelright Arms, a locals pub which was at one time a wheelright's but now concentrates on serving food and drink only.

Donkey Rides at Shortwood

24. PETERSTOW

This is an easy linear walk between Peterstow and Ross-on-Wye. The most difficult part is crossing the main A40 road when it is busy.

Distance: 3 miles (5 km)

Map: Pathfinder Sheet 1064 Ross-on-Wye (West)

How To Get There:

By Bus: Travel on the Red and White 38 bus between Gloucester and Hereford. The bus is hourly from Mondays to Saturdays but less frequent on Sunday afternoon and evening. The stop in the Hereford direction is by the village green and in the opposite direction by the shop and post office.

By Car: Park in Ross-on-Wye, at the riverside car park, then catch the bus from Cantelupe Street, or by the Royal hotel or at Wilton across the River Wye.

Refreshment: Yew Tree Inn at Peterstow. There are several cafes and pubs in Ross and inns at Wilton on the latter part of the walk.

Nearest Tourist Information: 20 Broad St, Ross-on-Wye. Tel: (0989) 62768

Peterstow has an attractive smell when the freshly baked bread is on sale at the Post Office and stores: a focal point of the village nestled around the old common with its good looking chestnut tree and old pump nearby. The village was at one time a gateway to a group of large farms but these have been sold or amalgamated in recent years. The church is mainly Victorian but originally dates from Norman times. It is in a lovely setting and a detour can be made on the walk to visit it and also a local farm just down the road.

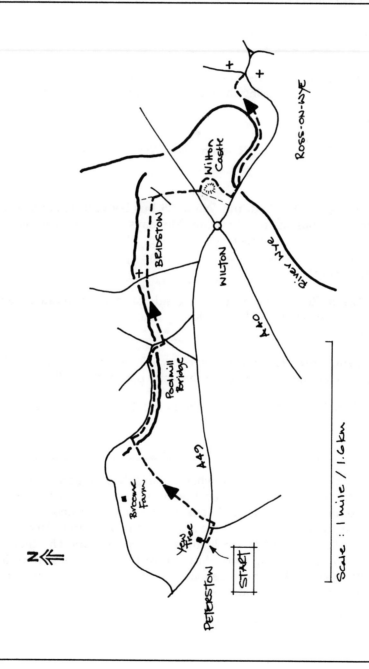

Broome Farm

Broome farm, not only offers accommodation and cream teas but also makes a delicious farmhouse cider from traditional orchards with varieties of apples with colourful names such as Foxwhelp and Yarlington mill. Go to the cellar when the cider is being drawn into half or gallon containers for the sight of rows of old whisky barrels now full of fermenting cider is most unusual. Nose the cider and sip carefully if taking a sample and at the very reasonable price of the product, a gallon will not exhaust the finances.

Start from the Yew Tree public house, one of the dwindling number of Whitbread houses in rural Herefordshire. Cross the road and turn left to walk along the pavement to a point just past the turning on the right. Cross the main road again and then go over the stile into a dry valley covered in rough pasture. Head slightly right to the next stile, cross it and then keep ahead with the hedge to your left, through a gateway and then slightly right towards several cottages.

St Bridgets' Church

Unless calling at Broome farm, which is a short way up the lane and on the left. Turn right this road shortly joins another. Go right and right again across Pool mill bridge then bear left over a stile by a gate, almost opposite a telephone kiosk. This path leads along a field's edge to St. Bridget's church at Bridstow, across the road and into the churchyard. Bridstow church dates from the twelfth century with much restoration in the fourteenth and nineteenth centuries. It is in a lovely setting and, as with many rural Herefordshire churches, it is a pleasure to dawdle awhile to reflect on life through the ages. The remains of the old cross indicate that it would have been of a large scale when intact.

Keep ahead through the churchyard, cross a stile and keep ahead once again on the slightly elevated ground. This path leads to a lane where you turn right. Within a few steps, turn left at the corner across a drive and into a field, keeping slightly right as you progress through the field at the rear of gardens. Perhaps, you have heard the noise, now here's the real challenge, the A40 with cars hurtling along at great pace. Please cross with extreme care as you require the agility of an air pilot to negotiate the weaving cars. Some local walkers simply give in and use the tunnel under the road instead which was presumably built for sheep and cattle rather than human beings and regain their route on the other side.

Wilton Castle

Once in the field on the other side of the main road head for the stile by the hedge surrounding Wilton castle, which happens to be private. There are two options here. Go left and follow the perimeter around to the right and onto the Wilton Bridge. The snag is that the plant life, lying so close to the River Wye grows to almost jungle proportions. The alternative is to forego the views of the castle ruins and cross the stile ahead. Walk along a narrow strip to cross a private drive, go through a kissing gate and drop down to another stile. keep ahead alongside the wall and go through a gate behind the Bridge House hotel, passing through the car park to the B4260 in Wilton. Across the road is The White Lion public house and further along The Wilton Court Hotel, both good places to stop for refreshment. The former was once a gaolhouse thought to be used as a prison by the lords of Wilton Court which was originally built as a courthouse in the sixteenth century.

Wilton castle has always been an attractive sort of castle, not really built for heavy military engagement and was eventually remodelled into a mansion. It was partly destroyed in the English Civil war and since has remained as gently decaying ivy clad ruins around a dwelling.

Turn left, unless visiting The White Lion or Wilton Court, cross the Wilton bridge and then turn left if walking back into Ross-on-Wye along the meadows. Wilton bridge dates from 1597, a blessing for local traders and travellers for so many of them got washed away in times of flood at this very difficult crossing point. There's an interesting eighteenth century sundial on the bridge with an inscription:

'Esteem thy precious time, which pass so swiftly away:

Prepare then for eternity and do not make delay'

Return into Ross-on-Wye by The Anchor public house before turning right and up to the Market Place.

25. RICHARD'S CASTLE

A lovely local walk from the village inn to Richard's castle and church standing high above the present day settlement. Fine views across the north of the county.

Distance: 3 miles

Map: Pathfinder sheets 972 Tenbury Wells and Mortimer's Cross and 951 Ludlow

How To Get There:

By Bus: Travel on the Midland Red 292 between Hereford, Leominster and Ludlow which stops by The Castle Inn in Richard's Castle.

By Car: Richard's Castle is on the B4361 road between Leominster and Ludlow. There is very limited car parking in and around the village, the safest point being close to the village hall just north of The Castle Inn.

Refreshment: The Castle Inn, Richard's Castle, a homely pub with host Katherine Cook serving a fine pint of Banks's bitter and snacks during the week as well as home prepared hot and cold food at weekends. The Castle Inn closes at 2 pm during weekday lunchtimes but is open all day Saturday.

Nearest Tourist Information: Castle Street, Ludlow, Shropshire SY8 1AS. Tel: (0584) 875053

Richard's Castle lies part in Herefordshire, part in Shropshire. The new church is seen on the B road from Ludlow and from here a narrow lane runs through to the old military settlement established by Richard Fitz Scrob, hence the name Richard's Castle. Historians note that this was an important borderland defensive site even before the invasion of William the Conqueror in 1066. Despite being used to quash local uprisings it was also a centre of commerce in mediaeval times and in 1216 it was granted a charter by King John to hold fairs and markets. By the fifteenth century the castle was in ruins and by the seventeenth century became the property of local gentry, The Salweys.

The history of the church is inextricably bound up with that of the castle for it was almost certainly built by Fitz Scrob or his son to serve the garrison and local community. There are few churches in Herefordshire with detached towers, Richard's Castle is one. Defence must have been the main consideration of the parishioners in this instance. The late thirteenth century detached tower would be used as a stronghold if necessary but given the way it was built, not with advantage against the

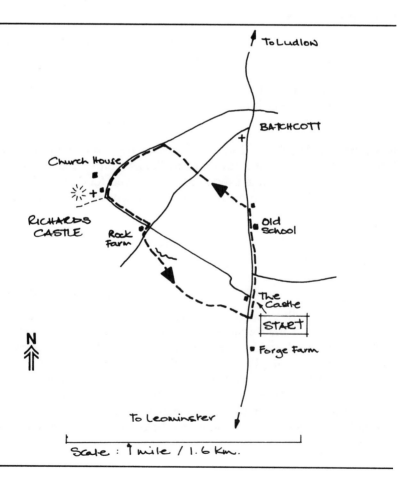

nearby castle. The church contains beautiful stained glass windows and many monuments and memorials.

From the entrance of The Castle Inn, turn left along the B4361 to pass the village hall and old school. Walk by another house and almost opposite a track and just before a half timbered cottage cross the road and go over a stile by a barred gate. Walk with the hedge to your left to cross an old 'V' stile. In the next field, head slightly left to the gate which brings you to a tarmac lane. The church to your right is in the hamlet of Batchcott in Shropshire for this is the boundary between the two counties.

The Church

Turn left and then immediately right to go through another gate. Head up the field ahead to a barred gate which leads to a parallel tarmac lane. Turn left to follow this quiet back lane to one of the loveliest parts of the county, Richard's Castle church standing by the earthworks of the fortress which once was so dominant.

Pass by Church cottage to a green kissing gate and into the churchyard. What a view across North Herefordshire. The choice of site was extremely judicious, for marching armies could be seen for miles around. Do take time to look at the church. A detailed guide book is available for a small donation.

Rock Farm

Retrace your steps to the lane but keep ahead down the hill to a cross roads. Turn right here, by Rock farm with the unusual intake steps into the upper floor. Go next left by a stream and cross the stile by the gate. Follow the hedge on the left to cross a track sandwiched by two stiles. Head slightly right across the field to stiles and a small bridge, rather like walking the plank, beneath a tree. Then, go left and choose the stile to the right. Cross this and another by the barred gate on the other side of a track. Proceed along the hedge on your left and finally exit into a lane by a cottage and ahead to the main road once again.

Forge Farm

No journey to Richard's Castle is complete without a call at the Forge Farm Cider company and do not be put off by the front yard which looks a bit of a jumble. The farm can be found on the main road, a little way to the right on the opposite side. This cider making farm is different as you have probably noticed already. The Evans's are welcoming people and you are encouraged to sample what is on offer before buying. Many a local will advise you to take care though as the cider which comes in medium or sweet varieties is powerful stuff. Take your own container preferably and given the very reasonable price it is usually sold in 2 litre bottles or more. There are also country wines and other products for sale. By the time you've had a glass or two of this you'll be singing the old farm hand's recitation often inscribed on the two handled 'God Speed The Plough' jars:

'Let the wealthy and the great
Roll in splendour and state
I envy them not I declare it
I eat my own lamb
My own chickens and ham
I shear my own fleece and wear it
I have lawns I have bowers
I have fruits I have flowers
The lark is my morning alarmer
So jolly boys now
Heres God speed the plough
Long life and success to the farmer'

26. STAUNTON on WYE

A walk to Monnington Ride returning by The Portway hotel and Staunton church. Gentle walking including a two miles of lanes.

Distance: 6-7 miles

Map: Pathfinder Sheet 1016 Hay-on-Wye

How To Get There:

By Bus: There is a Monday to Saturday service to Staunton on Wye from Hereford

By Car: Travel on the A438 road towards Hay-on-Wye and after the Portway Hotel there is a turning right by the youth hostel into the village where there is limited on street parking available.

Refreshment: The New Inn at Staunton. Your hosts, Barbara and Peter Clarke sell Theakstons Best Bitter and Brains SA as well as offering full meals and snacks at this friendly village pub. There is also a village stores.

Nearest Tourist Information: St. Owen Street, Hereford HR1 2PJ. Tel: (0432) 268430

Staunton-on-Wye, lying above the rich pastures of the River Wye is a village known to generations of youth hostellers who have come to stay on their walking or cycling tours through Herefordshire and into Wales. It is a village surrounded by fruit farming whether it be orchards, bush or soft fruit and this is the dominant form of agriculture on the south facing slopes around the village. The church is some distance from the settlement today, standing on a commanding site by an ancient farmhouse. It dates from Norman times but has been restored over the centuries.

Start from the New Inn. Go through the car park along a path between hedges to a stile leading into an orchard. Walk down the hill between trees and cross the two stiles ahead which lead into a small paddock. Go slightly right to follow the hedge around to a stile by a gate and down a track by houses to the main A438 road.

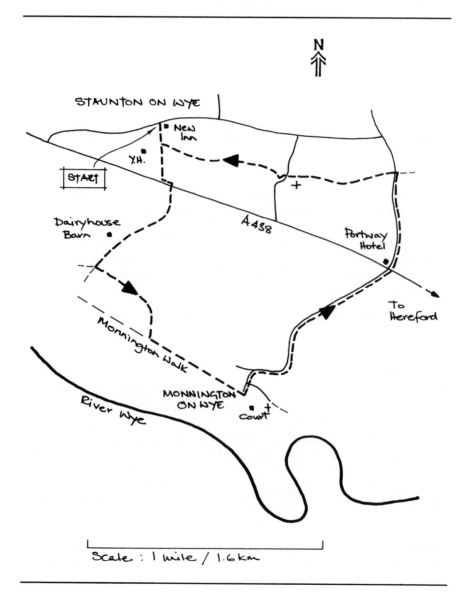

Scale : 1 mile / 1.6 km

Cross the road and through the gate signed as a bridleway, past the pavilion of Staunton FC to a gap in the hedge. Go through and head slightly right across the field to a gate and bridge over a stream. Keep ahead to another gate passing Dairyhouse barn to your right. Go through this and progress to the next gate but do not go through this time. Instead, turn left and follow the hedge on your right to the far corner where there is a gate to go through and a stile on the right to cross. The path leads to a wide green strip between trees, known as Monnington Walk or Ride.

Monnington Court

Turn left here and follow the green and then tarmac track towards Monnington Court and church. The court dates from the seventeenth century on the site of previous buildings belonging to the Monnington family. One story suggests that this was the final resting place of Welsh nationalist leader Owain Glyndŵr but this is hard to substantiate. Historians consider that it was feasible for Glyndŵr to have visited these parts as several of his daughters married into Herefordshire families but as to where he finally ended his days is conjecture.

The nearby church dates mainly from the seventeenth century financed by Uvedall and Mary Tomkins of Monnington Court and their initials are on the font. The woodwork is excellent, said to the work of John Abel, at one time a famous King's Carpenter to King Charles I and architect thought to be responsible for many important Herefordshire half-timbered houses. He is buried in Sarnesfield church near Weobley, the inscription on his tomb having been carved by himself at the age of ninety so it is said locally.

Before reaching the Court take the left turning and follow the road to another junction where you turn right and follow this for about a mile to the Portway hotel on the main road. Much of the land here is orcharded by Bulmers, a cider maker which leads the market.

Cross the main road at The Portway Hotel, recently closed and awaiting a new lease of life, hopefully. Keep ahead until you come to a right hand turn, signed as a bridleway and opposite a stile. Go over the stile, head slightly right to a stile beneath an oak and then head in a similar direction in the next field to cross another stile, climbing up towards

Staunton church. In the next field, head for the gate to the right of the church and follow the track down to the narrow lane by Staunton church.

The lane descends and before the corner, go right between a barn and shed along a track. This leads out into an open field planted with fruit. Follow the track as it veers left and down the field toward a cottage. As the track bends right here cross the stile on your left. As it is impossible to follow the exact path as shown on the map because of the close low level bushes, go right and then left up to the stile leading to the New Inn, heading diagonally right across the orchard. Perhaps, it is not the time to discuss fruit trees, but this is the way of modern fruit farming, dwarf or bush trees packed closely together in avenues which look so neat and tidy. Start of blossom is by far the best time to see them.

27. WALTERSTONE

A short walk in wild country along paths to Walterstone Camp and common returning to the Carpenter's Arms and Walterstone church

Distance: 3 miles

Map: Pathfinder Sheet Longtown and Pandy 1063

How To Get There:

By Bus: The nearest bus is on the Hereford to Abergavenny road at the Pandy Inn, a couple of miles away.

By Car: Travel on the A465 to the Pandy Inn at Pandy taking the right turn for Longtown. Take the first turn right for Walterstone. There is limited parking near the church and the pub.

Refreshment: The Carpenter's Arms is a splendid old pub which serves Wadsworth on draught in a homely surrounding where visitors are made welcome. It is a must for the walker. The Pandy Inn at Pandy is also very pleasant.

Nearest Tourist Information: Swan Meadow, Abergavenny, Gwent. Tel: (0873) 77588.

In Norman times Walterstone castle, a mound to be seen near to the church, must have been quite a busy borderland community. Now it is a quiet backwater which is predominantly farming country accustomed to a less bellicose way fo life. The church, standing on a piece of high ground near to the Carpenter's Arms and not much further away from the castle, offers superb views over to The Skirrid mountain. Well worth a climb while you are in this part of the county.

Hillfort

Start from the Carpenter's Arms. Turn left past the church and follow the tarmac lane down the hill. At the bottom, keep ahead to pass

Rockyfold along a farm track which leads up to Grove farm. At the rear of the farm walk up the green lane, partly overgrown to a barred gate at the top. Then go through the gap on the left as the main track continues uphill, across a field to the top right hand corner. To the right is Walterstone camp, an Iron Age hillfort which at a much later date in its history has been converted into a secret garden still to be seen although it is somewhat overgrown.

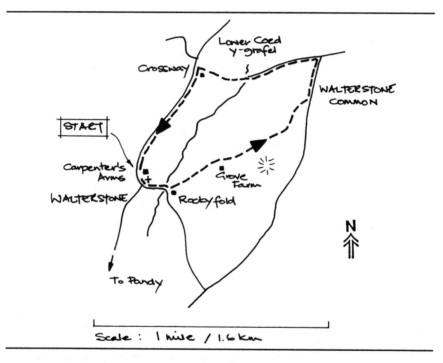

Go through the gate here, something of an obstacle course (and hopefully restiled shortly) and then left through another to walk through a small spinney and left along a rough narrow strip. Go slightly right as if to walk along another old track which is now full of scrub. Cut left into the field along a more frequently used path and right alongside the hedge to a gate which leads onto a tarmac lane by the old post office at Walterstone Common.

Common

Go left across the common by the old pump and to a lane running behind the old school. When planners talk of the decline of rural areas, these are places that show it in reality. The post office, school and bus have gone as the population has dwindled. The pub has only survived through persistence and hard work.

Join another track and turn left. This passes several lovely cottages as it begins to descend to Lower Coed-y-Grafel. The main track turns right to the farm but you continue down a sunken lane to a footbridge over the stream and up to a stile, a path reopened in recent years thanks to the campaigning of a local lady who enjoys walking. Cross this and head for the stile in the far left corner. Once over, keep ahead in a succession of fields with the hedge always to your left until you reach a tarmac lane just to the right of Crossways. Go left and follow the lane back to the Carpenter's Arms for well deserved refreshment.

28. WIGMORE

An exquisite walk through a very isolated part of Herefordshire to the village of Lingen. Walking in an area known as The Wigmore Rolls, steeped in history and legend. Several climbs but amply rewarded with views.

Distance: 11 miles but there is a cut off point after two miles.

Map: Pathfinder 972 Tenbury Wells and Mortimer's Cross and 971 Presteigne

How To Get There:

By Bus: With the utmost difficulty but there is a bus from Hereford which runs on college days to Wigmore in the morning and returns in the afternoon. Telephone (05473) 223 for timings.

By Car: Wigmore is on the A4110 road from Hereford to Knighton. There is limited on street parking in Wigmore.

Refreshment: The walker is fortunate here for not only is there a choice of an inn and hotel in Wigmore but also a public house in Lingen too. The Compasses Hotel in Wigmore offers accommodation breaks specifically geared to the walker and the landlord, Mike Crabtree, can arrange the services of local specialist guide or supply details for local self guided walks. Worthington Bitter is available on handpull and other guest beers are available throughout the year. Home cooked food is served at the bar or in the restaurant. Just down the road is the Olde Oak Inn, another welcoming hostelry, with hosts Ann and Peter Shaw, offering Banks's best bitter on draught and bar/restaurant meals. Near to the Olde Oak inn is the village stores which has a wide range of goods and repairs bicycles as well. What more could one ask for? Wigmore is a place to return to time and time again.

The Royal George at Lingen is a great place to take a rest mid way on the ramble (except Tuesday lunchtimes when it is closed). Jessica and Nicola Prosser sell draught beers from the Wood brewery in Shropshire as well as other guest beers in this lovely pub. Accommodation is available here and in nearby Brook Cottage. The George serves meals, snacks and takeaway food.

Nearest Tourist Information: Castle Street, Ludlow, Shropshire SY8 1AS. Tel: (0584) 875053.

Wigmore Castle

A local reverend writing about Wigmore in the earlier part of the century translated its old English name as 'the moor of the pirates'. It may well have been, for Wigmore was at one time a place of war and had some significance in English history. Wigmore castle became the seat of the imperialist, power seeking Mortimer family who ruled with an iron rod locally and influenced so many monarchs throughout the ages, embroiled in intrigue and betrayal. Can you imagine what the castle and village would have been like when host to great tournaments and fairs for the King's Council? It would have also been witness to many a bloody skirmish between English and Welsh or between the Marcher lords themselves seeking greater wealth by attacking their neighbours. The castle site was developed in the time of Alfred the Great's children but the ruins seen today belong to William Fitz Osborn. They were later passed on to Ralph de Mortimer. Some say what a pity more is not preserved. It is a majestic site but suffered badly during the English Civil wars.

The church is equally imposing, dating from Norman times with later improvements and full restoration in the last century. The church is known for the north wall of the nave which is a classic example of herringbone masonry.

Wigmore Abbey

Those seeking the ruins of Wigmore abbey will have to travel on to Adforton where this Augustinian enclave was established by one of the Mortimers in 1079 and subsequently became the burial ground for many of the family. Many of the stones from the abbey have since been incorporated in buildings throughout the parish, unfortunately for us but a good example of early recycling of materials.

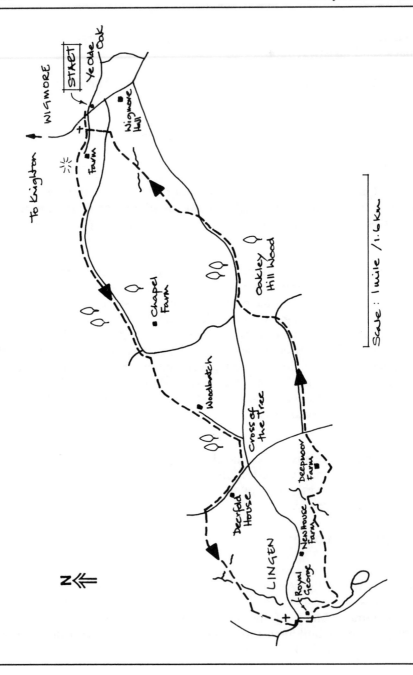

Start from Ye Olde Oak inn on the main road. Cross the road to pass by the furniture maker and walk along the road which continues beneath the church and the old school. Keep ahead but before Greenhill farm, follow the path rising to a gate and through a field to Wigmore castle. Drop back to the track which gives out into a field. Climb the steep bank pausing to look back at the strategic position of the castle and church. The path climbs to a stepped hedge on the left. Keep climbing up to cross a stile by a gate. In the next field go slightly left rising once again but with brilliant views across to Mortimers Forest. Cross the stile by the gate and then walk a few more steps to exit onto a tarmac lane. This is a possible cut off point by turning left and returning to Wigmore village.

Turn right and follow the road down a steep hill known as Tucknell bank and through woodland to a junction. The farm across the fields to the left is called Chapel farm, a solid early fifteenth century house thought at one time to be a secret place of worship for local followers of John Wycliffe, a leader of a group of religious reformers known as Lollards, prevalent in the fifteenth century.

Turn left and within a short distance go right up a green lane, known as Pig and Whistle. This climbs gently at first then dips into Woodbatch, one of the loveliest backwaters of the county, before climbing up once again to meet a road. Turn right and shortly right again at the road junction named Cross of the Tree, at one time the centre of a local Wesleyan following.

Deerfold

Pass Deerfold house and the road dips to a corner. Just beyond there is a stile on the left which you cross. Proceed down the batch but half way down begin to go slightly left along a feint green track to join the hedge and cross the stile here and another just beyond. Head towards the bottom left hand corner of the field and go over the drainage ditch. Walk ahead for a short distance through another gate and look for an indent in the field on the right which leads down to a ford across a brook and a recently provided footbridge.

Go slightly left to the corner of the field, through the barred gate and then left again after the water trough. Head for the church and cross the ditch before the castle mound by way of a bridge. Walk to the right of the ramparts and cross a stile into the churchyard. The castle, thought to have been of lesser importance in military terms was held by the Lingen family but fell into ruins early. The church stands alongside, dating from 1891 mainly as a fire destroyed the earlier building.

True Love

There's a lovely tale about a brave woman of the village who married local noble Grimbald, an arranged marriage. With a name like that, it must have been arranged. He immediately took off to fight against the Mohammedans in Tunis leaving his wife, poor Constantia, behind. Grimbald met with misfortune for he was captured and his ferocious Moorish captors insisted that he would remain prisoner forever unless his wife sacrificed a joint from her body in return for his freedom. Evidently, his beautiful wife severed her left hand above the wrist and had it transported to Africa where an astonished bunch of Moors released Grimbald to come home to Herefordshire where the couple lived happily ever after. An effigy of the couple is said to lie in Much Cowarne church near Pencombe.

South of the village lies the ruins of Limebrook nunnery established by one of the Lingen family in the early thirteenth century until its dissolution in the 1530s.

Royal George

Leave by way of a small gate to the right of the lych gate onto the road. Walk along the lane to call at The Royal George, a rather special pub which has doubled as a shop and post office. Just beyond the pub go left before a white cottage into a field. Keep ahead to pass between two healthy looking hawthorn bushes and cross a bridge over the brook. Keep company with the hedge on the right, to cross a stile and then go left over three footbridges giving out onto a track. Turn right but around the corner turn left through Oldcastle wood, presumably named after Sir John Oldcastle, a Lollard who took refuge in near Chapel farm during times of religious persecution. The path climbs and then curves right to exit by way of a gate into a meadow with New House farm to the left.

Go slightly left up the bank and through the gateway following the green track slightly left and then ahead climbing gently across the shoulder of the field to a barred gate. Once through go right down the hill and in a short while look for a track turning right across the stream but be careful to bear left up an old track, which can get brambly, up to a gate. Keep ahead and climb up to another gate and into a wooded section and up to an aggregate track. Bear left at the next main junction with Deepmoor farm to your left over the field. Follow this lane to a tarmac road.

Mistletoe

Keep ahead and soak up the views as you descend to a corner. Proceed straight ahead along the rough track which curves left by an orchard known as Mistletoe Oak, possibly a reference to the saphrophyte very rarely using an oak as its host. It usually lives with the apple tree and Herefordshire is the world centre for mistletoe, not only because the county is full of romantics but as a by product of the orchard. Tenbury Wells is the biggest marketplace for mistletoe in the world, although traders are worried that it is dying out with the decline in old orchards.

The track then climbs gently to another road. Turn right and climb up through Oakley hill wood for over half a mile with interesting roadside flora including wild strawberries. The woodland begins to open up on the left and, as the road curves right, your way is left over a stile into a field. Cut across slightly right to the wood's corner and then head for the top right corner where you go through a gate. Turn right to follow the hedge for the best part of the field before cutting left to go through a gate.

Wigmore Hall

Walk slightly left across this next field to cross another stile leading into a dry valley and offering fine views in the direction of Ludlow. Walk down the valley to a footbridge across the stream and then go right at first. However, begin to bear slightly left as you climb up the bank through parkland and with views of Wigmore Hall, a distinctive looking half timbered country dwelling, in the distance. Keep climbing until the field levels and look for the footpath signpost as a landmark.

Exit here into a lane, turn right and within a very short distance cross a stile on the left. Walk alongside the hedge to cross another stile and then follow the narrow track down the hill to a stream. Turn right at first and then left to bring you up to the road used on the outward section. By all means divert by way fo the church as there is a path through the churchyard and back to the centre of the village.

29. WOOLHOPE

By far the prettiest village in the Woolhope Dome area with a ramble across fields to Sollers Hope and Gurney's Oak returning through the quiet pastures of Alford Mill.

Distance: 7 miles

Map: Pathfinder sheet 1041 Ledbury and Much Marcle

How To Get There:

By Bus: There is a limited Monday to Saturday service from Hereford to Woolhope.

By Car: Travel on the B4224 to Mordiford and turn left after the Moon inn on the road through Haugh Wood to Woolhope. The amount of parking in and around the village is limited so please park tidily.

Refreshment: The Crown Inn at Woolhope is not only renowned for its good cooking but also sells a great pint of Smiles, an appropriate name for the beer which is brewed in Bristol. Just outside the village is another old Herefordshire pub, The Butchers which also sells good draught beer and serves food. The Butchers Arms is CAMRA recommended. The Gurney's Oak usually has a handpulled beer available and is approximately the half way point on the ramble.

Nearest Tourist Information: St. Owens Street, Hereford HR1 2PJ. Tel: (0432) 268430

Who would have thought that this village is connected with the lady of flowing hair and naked body, Lady Godiva. It was her sister, Wulviva, who perhaps gave her name to the area -'Wulviva's Hope'. The sisters gave Woolhope to the Bishops of Hereford who at one time or another seemed to amass considerable tracts of land throughout the county.

Woolhope is well known to geologists and naturalists, including that marvellous Woolhope Club – started in 1851 and having since

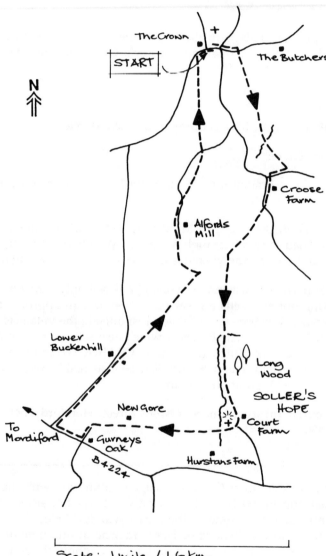

N

The Crown

START

The Butchers

Croose Farm

Alfords Mill

Lower Buckenhill

Long Wood

SOLLER'S HOPE

New Gore

To Mordiford

Gurneys Oak

B 4224

Court Farm

Hurstans Farm

Scale: 1 mile / 1.6 km.

researched so much material about the county. The Woolhope Dome, is in simple terms, an eroded dome with an upwards thrust of older Silurian limestones and shales exposed by thousands of years of weathering. The area is predominantly under pasture but with orchards and woodland throughout. The gentle ripples of the landscape broken by meandering streams makes it such pleasant walking.

The Wonder

Start from the entrance to the church. Turn left and then downhill along the Putley road, passing the telephone kiosk and then Stone house. After the last building on the right cross a stile which looks more like fencing and walk along the fence ahead to another stile. There are good views of Marcle Ridge from here, a feature to be admired throughout the route. Marcle Ridge has been known to scare the locals silly, for it has a habit of slipping. On a cold February day in 1575, there was a massive earth movement which continued for three days destroying all around including the then chapel of Kynaston. The story is that the chapel's bell was ploughed up centuries later and is now at Homme house near Ledbury. The landslip has been known as 'The Wonder' to this day.

On the other side of the hill is Putley, the centre of the Big Apple event which has occurred in recent years, very much a community event where the virtues and qualities of apples are extolled with apple tastings, identification of rare varieties, apples in cooking demonstrations and such like are organised over several weekends in late autumn.

Go slightly left across this next field to a clearing and pass by the remains of a corrugated barn to a stile. Cross here and then go right at first but then cut left across the field to a stile. Once over, turn immediately right to cross another stile into an orchard. Then head diagonally left, missing the trees of course, to a footbridge which you cross.

Head across the field towards two isolated trees ahead and with the ancient Croose farm to your right. Exit onto the lane, turn right and at the triangular junction go left. After the road bends left, look for the low level white metal fencing. This is the right of way (some use the gate nearby). Go over by the pole and head directly across the field, passing by the middle electric telegraph pole to a gap in the line of trees sheltering the drainage ditch. Cross here and keep ahead through a narrow meadow to cross another stile and then ahead to pass through a gateway and proceed ahead once again with Long wood to the left and the stream to the right.

Pass through another gateway mid field now with Sollers Hope church and Court farm clearly in view. What a magnificent rural enclave, with no finer view than approaching from this direction on foot.

Sollers Hope

As you approach the farm buildings go through the gateway on the left which leads through the farmyard to the tarmac lane beyond the house. Enter the churchyard. This fine old church, with restored cross in the churchyard has been the subject of much affection over the centuries by its parishioners. There is an interesting Norman font in the church and also several tombstones, including one coffin lid which has engraved on it the arms of the Solers family.

Dick Whittington

The amazing feature of the church is that much of the roofing and adjoining woodwork is original, having been covered by plaster over the years until 1887 when the church received a degree of restoration. One tale which intrigues the walker is the association of Dick Whittington with this out of the way chapel miles from London. Some actually say he was born here but are less sure about the cat. Evidently, Dick's brother Robert Whittington, financed the restoration of an earlier Anglo Saxon church on the site in the fourteenth century. What a splendid achievement as the church you see today is very much a mediaeval triumph in design.

Pass by the church to a gate leading out into a narrow strip of land and to a footbridge. From here you obtain a better view of an old motte reflecting the strategic importance of the site in earlier times. The fort would have been of wood originally and therefore little or no stonework would have existed. It would have become derelict as the borderlands settled into a less aggressive way of life.

Climb the bank away from the church and with Hurstans farm to the left. Cross a stile and keep company with the field boundary on the left, with views over to Woolhope church on your right. Go left over a stile and then right continuing ahead once again, with a house to your right. Cross the barred gate part way along onto a track, and then go left.

Gurney's Oak

This leads down to The Gurney's Oak public house, an interesting old house selling a wide range of drinks including one or two real ales. Turn right onto the B4224 and then right at the first junction. Walk along this lane to pass Lower Buckenhill farm and just beyond as the road rises cross wooden rails into the field and turn left to walk near to the hedge to the brow and through a gateway. Go right across this next field down towards a hedge curving in a semi circle but then going slightly right to a gateway. Once through go slightly right to a stile and cross it and then

The Crown at Woolhope

keep ahead to a gate leading to Alfords Mill, although the right of way should cut through the hedge near to the footbridge seen to your right.

Walk up the lane and as it bends sharply left, keep ahead through the gateway as signed. The field corner drops away right but continue straight ahead over the field to cross a stile. In the next field head slightly left to cross another stile which leads onto the lane. Cross the stile on the other side, turn right and walk through the narrow field to a stile which is crossed and then keep ahead with the hedge on your right to meet a tarmac lane, turn left to return to Woolhope village.

30. YARPOLE

A walk between the historic villages of Yarpole and Bircher by way of Bircher Common with great views across the Lugg plain

Distance: 5 miles

Map: Pathfinder sheet 972 Tenbury Wells and Mortimers Cross

How To Get There:

By Bus: There is a very limited service on Tuesdays and Fridays from Leominster to Yarpole and Bircher provided by Midland Red West and Lugg Valley motors.

By Car: Travel on the B4361 between Leominster and Ludlow. After Luston look for a turning to the left for Yarpole. After a mile turn right at the junction for Yarpole. In the village turn left and there is limited parking near the church and Bell inn but park considerately.

Refreshment: The Bell at Yarpole sells a good pint of Woods beer in pleasant surroundings and serves food. The Tea Rooms at Yarpole Stores, which is a shop, home bakery and cafe all in one, are open during the summer.

Nearest Tourist Information: 6 School Lane, Leominster HR6 8AA. Tel: (0568) 6460

Yarpole church contains a magnificent fourteenth century detached bell tower, a wooden structure with a stone outer wall. The rest of the church dates from the twelfth and thirteenth century with later restorations and is well worth a visit. Yarpole, the name meaning the damming of a stream and pool, is a homely village with several historic buildings nestled in and around the brook.

Nearby is Croft castle, a house dating from the sixteenth century and on the site of former halls, as well as Croft Ambrey hillfort. Both are owned by the National Trust and therefore open to the public. It is possible to combine this walk with a visit to these places in one day.

Start the walk from The Bell Inn. Turn left and at the junction by Yarpole stores left again. Just beyond the last house on the left, Brick House, go through a barred gate. Walk along the old green track to a point just beyond the field corner to cross a stile, hidden at first, beneath an elderberry tree. In the next field keep ahead and cross another stile. Keep in a similar direction but making for a stile closer to the stream in the top tapering corner of the field. Cross this and walk up to the gap in the hedge, then proceeding to a stile leading onto the road.

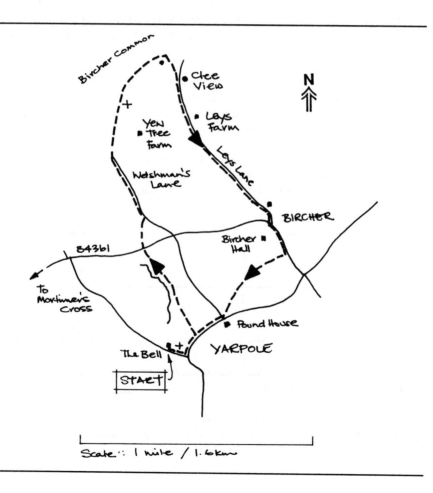

Welshman's Lane

Go over the road, cross the stile and your way is alongside this hedge until you reach a tarmac lane known as Welshman's lane: a reminder that this is truly border country and where England met Wales was not as clear as the political boundaries concocted in the twentieth century.

Turn left up the lane to Bircher Common, across the cattle grid by the bus shelter with its very own kissing gate. Head uphill to the right across the bracken clad common, now owned by the National Trust. Pass to the left of the chapel and once beyond the house at the corner go right and walk along the common's edge to the last house, Rambler's Retreat. Here you make a turn right and walk downhill to Leys lane where you turn right and follow it to the main road, once again, in Bircher.

Bircher

What a good looking hamlet this is with beautifully restored buildings to the right, Bircher hall and other sturdy houses. Walk ahead along the pavement but well before the corner cross the road and a stile by a farm entrance. Cross another in close succession before heading slightly right to another stile and on to another by four tall spruce trees. Go over the stile here and walk by the hedge down the field to another stile and ahead once again to the right of the barn and onto a lane.

Turn left and immediately right, passing by the Pound House, an old farmhouse, no doubt, at one time a place for collecting rents and dues in the parish. The lane leads into Yarpole, one of North Herefordshire's best kept secrets and just the place to stay awhile.